THE BOOK OF
VEGETARIAN
COOKING

THE BOOK OF
VEGETARIAN
COOKING

TED SMART

Specially produced for Ted Smart,
Guardian House, Borough Road,
Godalming, Surrey GU7 2AE

ISBN 1 85613 036 3

CREDITS

Designer: Sara Cooper

Contributing authors: June Budgen, Sarah Bush, Linda Fraser,
Annette Grimsdale, Gordon Grimsdale, Kerenza Harries,
Lesley Mackley, Janice Murfitt, Mary Norwak, Lorna Rhodes,
Louise Steele, Sally Taylor

Typeset: Maron Graphics Ltd., Wembley

Colour separation by: Fotographics Ltd., J. Film Process Ltd.,
Kentscan Ltd., Magnum Graphics Ltd., Scantrans Pte. Ltd.

Photographers: Simon Butcher, Per Ericson, David Gill,
Paul Grater, Sue Jorgensen, Ray Joyce, Alan Newnham, Jon Stewart,
Alister Thorpe

Printed in Italy

CONTENTS

FENNEL & WALNUT SOUP

3 teaspoons vegetable oil
1 onion, chopped
1 large bulb fennel, trimmed and chopped
940 ml (1½ pints/3¾ cups) vegetable stock
60 g (2 oz/½ cup) chopped walnuts

SAGE DERBY PUFFS: 30 g (1 oz/6 teaspoons) butter
30 g (1 oz/¼ cup) plain flour
½ egg, beaten
90 g (3 oz) Sage Derby cheese grated
salt and pepper
60 g (2 oz/¼ cup) cream cheese
6 teaspoons single (light) cream

To make puffs, preheat oven to 200C (400F/ Gas 6). Put butter and 45 ml (1½ fl oz/9 teaspoons) water into a saucepan and bring to the boil. Add flour off heat and beat until smooth. Cool slightly, then beat in egg and add half Sage Derby and salt and pepper. Put into a piping bag fitted with small plain nozzle and pipe blobs the size of peas on to a greased baking tray. Bake 7-10 minutes, until crisp. Cool slightly, then slit each. To make soup, heat oil in a pan, add onion and fennel and cook until soft. Add stock, bring to boil, then simmer, covered, for 20 minutes.

Meanwhile, beat remaining cheese with cream cheese and cream. Fill pastry puffs. Grind three-quarters of the walnuts in a blender or food processor; chop the rest and reserve for garnish. Purée soup until smooth, then return to pan and stir in ground nuts and add salt and pepper. Reheat gently. Serve garnished with Sage Derby puffs and sprinkled with reserved walnuts.

Serves 4-6.

WATERCRESS & ALMOND SOUP

2 large bunches watercress
30 g (1 oz/6 teaspoons) butter
1 small onion, finely chopped
500 ml (16 fl oz/2 cups) vegetable stock
60 g (2 oz/⅓ cup) blanched almonds, toasted and ground
4 teaspoons cornflour
500 ml (16 fl oz/2 cups) milk
salt and pepper
flaked almonds, lightly toasted, to garnish

Wash watercress and reserve a few sprigs for garnish. Cut away any coarse stalks and chop remainder.

Melt butter in a saucepan, add onion and cook gently until soft. Add watercress and cook for 2 minutes, then stir in stock, cover and simmer for 10 minutes.

Purée in a blender or food processor and return to rinsed out pan with the ground almonds. Blend cornflour with a little of the milk, then add to pan with remaining milk and cook gently over a low heat for 5 minutes, stirring, until smooth. Remove from heat and set aside to cool. Refrigerate for at least 4 hours or overnight. Season, then serve garnished with a few toasted flaked almonds sprinkled on top and the reserved watercress sprigs.

Serves 4.

TOMATO & RICE SOUP

CELERY & STILTON SOUP

1 small onion, chopped
2 cloves garlic, crushed
794 g (1 lb 12 oz) can tomatoes
6 teaspoons tomato purée (paste)
3 teaspoons chopped fresh basil or ½ teaspoon dried
1 teaspoon sugar
60 g (2 oz/⅓ cup) long-grain rice
9 teaspoons dry sherry
salt and pepper
9 teaspoons single (light) cream and basil leaves, to garnish, if desired

1 head celery
45 g (1½ oz/9 teaspoons) butter
1 onion, chopped
940 ml (1½ pints/3¾ cups) light vegetable stock
2 egg yolks
155 ml (5 fl oz/⅔ cup) single (light) cream
125 g (4 oz) blue Stilton, rinded and crumbled
salt and pepper

BLUE CHEESE CROÛTONS 30 g (1 oz/6 teaspoons) butter, softened
30 g (1 oz) blue cheese, grated
1 thick slice bread

Put onion, garlic, tomatoes with their juice, tomato purée (paste), basil, sugar and 625 ml (20 fl oz/2½ cups) water into a saucepan. Bring to the boil, cover and simmer for 30 minutes. Pour into a blender or food processor and purée. Sieve purée back into pan.

Reserve inner leaves from celery and chop remainder. Melt butter in a large saucepan, add celery and onion, then cover and cook gently, until soft. Add stock, bring to the boil, re-cover and simmer 20 minutes or until vegetables are tender. Cool slightly, then purée in a blender or food processor. Return soup to rinsed-out pan and reheat gently: do not boil.

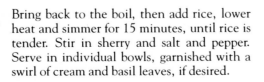

Bring back to the boil, then add rice, lower heat and simmer for 15 minutes, until rice is tender. Stir in sherry and salt and pepper. Serve in individual bowls, garnished with a swirl of cream and basil leaves, if desired.

Serves 4-6.

Meanwhile, make croûtons. Beat butter and cheese together. Toast bread and spread cheese butter on 1 side, then grill until melted. Cut into squares. To finish soup, beat egg yolks and cream together. Stir a small ladleful of soup into egg mixture and pour back into pan. Stir in cheese, stirring until thick. Season if needed. Serve hot with croûtons and garnished with reserved celery leaves.

Serves 4-6.

SPICY LENTIL SOUP

MEXICAN BEAN SOUP

6 teaspoons olive oil
½ teaspoon cumin seeds
1 onion, chopped
1 clove garlic, crushed
2 carrots, chopped
2 sticks celery, chopped
½ teaspoon chilli powder
½ teaspoon turmeric
1 teaspoon ground coriander
185 g (6 oz) red lentils, washed and picked over
1.2 litres (2 pints/5 cups) vegetable stock
1 bay leaf
salt and pepper
fried onion rings and coriander leaves, to garnish

6 teaspoons olive oil
1 onion, chopped
1 clove garlic, crushed
1 green pepper (capsicum), seeded and diced
375 g (12 oz) tomatoes, skinned and chopped
½ teaspoon chilli powder
940 ml (1½ pints/3¾ cups) vegetable stock
6 teaspoons tomato purée (paste)
470 g (15 oz) can red kidney beans, drained
salt and pepper
125 g (4 oz) canned sweetcorn
1 avocado
few drops Tabasco sauce
1 tablespoon chopped fresh coriander
coriander leaves, to garnish

Heat oil in a saucepan over a medium heat; add cumin seeds. As soon as seeds begin to pop, add onion and cook until golden, stirring. Add garlic, carrots and celery and cook gently for 10 minutes, until soft. Stir in all the spices and cook for a further 1 minute before adding lentils.

Heat oil in a large saucepan and cook onion until soft. Add garlic, green pepper (capsicum), tomatoes and chilli powder and cook for 3-4 minutes. Pour in stock with tomato purée (paste) and three-quarters of the beans. Re-cover and simmer for 30 minutes, then cool slightly and purée in a blender or food processor.

Pour in stock and bay leaf and bring to the boil, then simmer for 1 hour, skimming surface if necessary. Remove bay leaf and purée soup in a blender or food processor. Return to pan, season with salt and pepper and reheat. Serve garnished with fried onion rings and coriander leaves.

Serves 6.

Return to pan and add salt and pepper, remaining beans and sweetcorn. Peel and dice avocado and add with the Tabasco sauce. Reheat gently, stir in coriander and serve garnished with coriander leaves.

Serves 4-5.

POTAGE BONNE FEMME

HARVEST BARLEY SOUP

60 g (2 oz/¼ cup) butter
500 g (1 lb) potatoes, diced
2 carrots, chopped
2 large leeks, trimmed and chopped
940 ml (1½ pints/3¾ cups) vegetable stock
salt and pepper
125 ml (4 fl oz/½ cup) double (thick) cream
1 tablespoon finely chopped fresh parsley or chervil

TO GARNISH: ½ carrot, cut into fine strips
½ small leek, cut into fine strips
1 slice bread, toasted

Melt butter in a saucepan and add prepared vegetables.

Cover and cook gently for 15 minutes. Add stock and bring to the boil, then re-cover and simmer for 20 minutes. Purée in a blender or food processor, then press through a sieve. Return soup to pan, add salt and pepper and stir in cream and parsley or chervil. Reheat very gently.

To make garnish, blanch the fine strips of carrot and leek in a pan for 1 minute, then drain. Cut out 4 small rounds of toast and divide the vegetables between them. Float on top of individual bowls of hot soup.

Serves 4.

60 g (2 oz/⅓ cup) pearl barley
1.2 litres (2 pints/5 cups) vegetable stock
1 large carrot, diced
1 small turnip, diced
1 stick celery, chopped
1 small onion, finely chopped
2 young leeks, trimmed and sliced
½ teaspoon mixed dried herbs and 1 bay leaf
5 teaspoons tomato purée (paste)
salt and pepper
230 g (7½ oz) can butter beans, drained and rinsed

CHEESY CROÛTONS: 1 thick slice bread
60 g (2 oz/½ cup) Cheddar cheese, grated

Put barley into a saucepan with stock and bring to the boil, then cover and simmer for 45 minutes, until barley is tender. Add vegetables, herbs, tomato purée (paste) and salt and pepper and simmer, covered, for 20 minutes. Meanwhile, make croûtons. Toast bread on both sides, remove crusts and scatter cheese over the bread. Grill until melted and golden. Cut into squares.

Remove bay leaf from soup, stir in beans and cook gently for 5 minutes to heat through. Garnish the soup with the croûtons and serve at once.

Serves 4-6.

— COURGETTE & TOMATO SOUP —

30 g (1 oz/6 teaspoons) butter
1 onion, finely chopped
375 g (12 oz) courgettes (zucchini), coarsely grated
1 clove garlic, crushed
625 ml (20 fl oz/2½ cups) vegetable stock
440 g (14 oz) can chopped tomatoes
2 tablespoons chopped fresh mixed herbs, if desired
salt and pepper
60 ml (2 fl oz/¼ cup) double (thick) cream and basil leaves, to garnish

Melt butter in a saucepan, add onion and cook until soft. Add courgettes (zucchini) and garlic and cook for 4-5 minutes.

Add stock and tomatoes with their juice, then bring to the boil, cover and simmer for 15 minutes.

Stir in herbs, if desired, and salt and pepper. Serve the soup in individual bowls, garnished with teaspoonfuls of cream stirred in or floating on the surface and basil leaves.

Serves 4.

— MINORCAN VEGETABLE SOUP —

2 red peppers (capsicums)
6 teaspoons olive oil
1 large Spanish onion
2 cloves garlic, finely chopped
250 g (8 oz) tomatoes, skinned, seeded and chopped
1 small cabbage
½ teaspoon dried thyme
1 bay leaf
1 teaspoon paprika
salt and pepper
4-6 thick slices bread, toasted
2 cloves garlic, halved

Place peppers (capsicums) under grill and turn until charred.

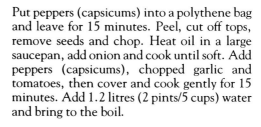

Put peppers (capsicums) into a polythene bag and leave for 15 minutes. Peel, cut off tops, remove seeds and chop. Heat oil in a large saucepan, add onion and cook until soft. Add peppers (capsicums), chopped garlic and tomatoes, then cover and cook gently for 15 minutes. Add 1.2 litres (2 pints/5 cups) water and bring to the boil.

Discard outside leaves from cabbage, then shred and add to soup with thyme, bay leaf and paprika and simmer for 15 minutes. Season with salt and pepper. Rub toast with a cut side of garlic. Lay a slice of toast in each soup plate, then ladle over the hot soup. Serve at once.

Serves 4-6.

CREAM OF CARROT SOUP

TARRAGON & TOMATO SOUP

60 g (2 oz/¼ cup) butter
1 small onion, finely chopped
1 potato, diced
500 g (1 lb) carrots, chopped
750 ml (24 fl oz/3 cups) vegetable stock
pinch sugar
155 ml (5 fl oz/⅔ cup) single (light) cream
salt and pepper

HERBY CROÛTONS: 1 teaspoon dried mixed herbs
2 slices bread

90 g (3 oz) bunch sorrel leaves
500 g (1 lb) ripe tomatoes
6 teaspoons olive oil
1 small onion, chopped
500 ml (16 fl oz/2 cups) vegetable stock
155 ml (5 fl oz/⅔ cup) dry white wine
2 egg yolks
155 ml (5 fl oz/⅔ cup) single (light) cream
salt and pepper
1 tablespoon chopped fresh tarragon
extra cream and fresh tarragon, to garnish

Melt half the butter in a saucepan. Add onion, potato and carrots.

Trim stalks from sorrel and chop tomatoes. Heat oil, add onion and cook until soft.

Cover and cook over low heat for 10 minutes. Add stock and sugar and bring to the boil, then cover and simmer for 30 minutes. Purée in a blender or food processor, then return to pan and add cream. Add salt and pepper.

Add sorrel and tomatoes and cook for a further 15 minutes over a very low heat. Add stock and wine and cook for a further 10 minutes. Press the soup through a sieve into a clean pan.

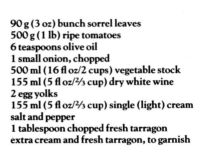

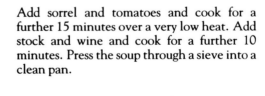

To make croûtons, preheat oven to 200C (400F/Gas 6). Beat remaining butter and the mixed herbs together, then spread over bread. Cut into fancy shapes or squares and place on a baking tray. Bake until crisp and golden. Serve with the soup.

Serves 4.

Beat egg yolks and cream together and ladle in a little soup, then mix together. Pour back into pan and reheat to thicken. Add salt and pepper and stir in tarragon. Serve garnished with a swirl of cream and a tiny sprig of tarragon.

Serves 4-6.

CARROT & CORIANDER SOUP

500 g (1 lb) carrots
6 teaspoons olive oil
1 small onion, finely chopped
1 clove garlic, crushed
1 teaspoon coriander seeds, crushed
1 teaspoon ground coriander
940 ml (1½ pints/3¾ cups) vegetable stock
60 g (2 oz/⅓ cup) sultanas, chopped
salt and pepper
1 tablespoon chopped fresh coriander leaves

SESAME CROÛTONS: 1 thick slice bread, crusts removed
15 g (½ oz/3 teaspoons) butter
3 teaspoons sesame seeds

Cut 2 carrots into small dice and set aside. Chop remaining carrots. Heat oil in a large saucepan, add onion, garlic and chopped carrots and cook gently for 10 minutes. Stir in crushed and ground coriander and cook for 1 minute. Add 750 ml (24 fl oz/3 cups) of the stock, cover and simmer for 15 minutes, or until the carrots are tender. Meanwhile, put diced carrots in a small saucepan with remaining stock and simmer until tender.

Purée soup in a blender or food processor, then return to pan. Add diced carrots, sultanas and salt and pepper. Reheat gently while making the croûtons. Toast bread on each side until golden. Cool, then spread with butter and sprinkle over sesame seeds. Return to grill until golden. Cut into small cubes. To serve, stir in chopped coriander and garnish with sesame seed croûtons.

Serves 4.

FRENCH TURNIP SOUP

30 g (1 oz/6 teaspoons) butter
500 g (1 lb) small white turnips, chopped
1 small onion, chopped
1.2 litres (2 pints/5 cups) vegetable stock
4 slices white bread, crusts removed
125 g (4 oz) shelled fresh peas
salt and pepper
pinch grated nutmeg

CHEESY PUFFS: 125 g (4 oz) puff pastry, thawed if frozen
45 g (1½ oz/9 teaspoons) cream cheese with herbs and garlic
1 egg, beaten, to glaze

Melt butter in a pan, add turnips and onion.

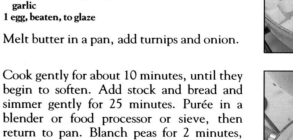

Cook gently for about 10 minutes, until they begin to soften. Add stock and bread and simmer gently for 25 minutes. Purée in a blender or food processor or sieve, then return to pan. Blanch peas for 2 minutes, then add to soup with salt and pepper and nutmeg.

To make garnish, preheat oven to 200C (400F/Gas 6). Roll out pastry thinly and cut into 5 cm (2 in) rounds. Place ½ teaspoon of cheese in each centre, dampen edges, fold over and place on a greased baking tray. Brush with beaten egg, then bake in the oven until crisp and golden. Float them on the hot soup when ready to serve.

Serves 4.

CLEAR VEGETABLE SOUP

WINTER VEGETABLE BROTH

2 young carrots, thinly sliced
2 sticks celery, sliced
60 g (2 oz) button mushrooms, sliced
125 g (4 oz) broccoli flowerets
45 g (1½ oz) frozen peas
1 courgette (zucchini), cut into thin strips

VEGETABLE STOCK: 1 small onion, thinly sliced
1 leek, chopped
2 sticks celery, chopped
3 carrots, chopped
2 tomatoes, chopped
bouquet garni
2 bay leaves
salt
½ teaspoon black peppercorns

30 g (1 oz/6 teaspoons) butter
1 onion, sliced
250 g (8 oz) carrots, diced
250 g (8 oz) swede, diced
1 potato, diced
2 large parsnips, diced
500 ml (16 fl oz/2 cups) vegetable stock
1 bay leaf
3 teaspoons cornflour
500 ml (16 fl oz/2 cups) milk
salt and pepper
90 g (3 oz) frozen peas
2 small bread rolls and 60 g (2 oz/½ cup) Cheddar
    cheese, grated, to garnish

To make stock, put all ingredients into a saucepan, add 1.2 litres (2 pints/5 cups) water. Bring to the boil and simmer for 40 minutes, then strain; this stock does not need degreasing. For a stronger flavour, boil rapidly for 5 minutes to reduce to 940 ml (1½ pints/ 3¾ cups). Put the stock into rinsed-out pan, add sliced carrots, celery, mushrooms and broccoli. Bring to the boil, cover and simmer for 5 minutes.

Melt butter in a saucepan, add vegetables, except peas, cover and cook gently for 10 minutes. Add stock and bay leaf, re-cover and simmer for 30 minutes. Blend cornflour with a little milk, then add to soup with remaining milk and cook, stirring until thickened. Remove bay leaf and add salt and pepper.

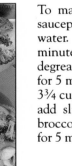

Stir in peas and courgettes (zucchini) and cook for a further 2 minutes. Season to taste before serving.

Serves 4.

Stir peas into soup and simmer for 2-3 minutes while making garnish. Cut bread rolls in half, divide the cheese between them and grill until melted. Place on top of each portion of soup just before serving.

Serves 4.

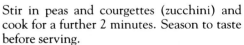

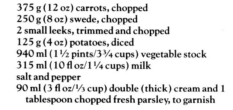

CELERY & ONION SOUP

1 head celery
2 onions
60 (2 oz/¼ cup) butter
3 teaspoons plain flour
750 ml (24 fl oz/3 cups) milk
1 bay leaf
60 ml (2 fl oz/¼ cup) crème fraîche
salt and pepper

Take 1 stick of celery and cut into thin strips, place in a bowl of iced water and set aside. Reserve a few leaves for garnish. Reserve one quarter of an onion, then chop remaining onion and celery.

Melt butter in a saucepan, add onion and celery and cook for 5 minutes. Stir in flour and cook for 1 minute, then gradually stir in milk. Add bay leaf, cover and simmer for 20 minutes.

Cool slightly, remove bay leaf, then purée soup in a blender or food processor. Return to pan, stir in crème fraîche and add salt and pepper. Reheat gently. Chop reserved onion and add to soup. Drain celery curls and use to garnish soup with reserved leaves.

Serves 4-6.

GOLDEN VEGETABLE SOUP

375 g (12 oz) carrots, chopped
250 g (8 oz) swede, chopped
2 small leeks, trimmed and chopped
125 g (4 oz) potatoes, diced
940 ml (1½ pints/3¾ cups) vegetable stock
315 ml (10 fl oz/1¼ cups) milk
salt and pepper
90 ml (3 fl oz/⅓ cup) double (thick) cream and 1
  tablespoon chopped fresh parsley, to garnish

Put all the vegetables in a large saucepan, add stock and bring to the boil. Cover and simmer for 30 minutes, until tender.

Purée in a blender or food processor, then return to rinsed-out pan and stir in milk. Reheat and add salt and pepper.

When ready to serve, whip cream until holding its shape and stir in parsley. Float a spoonful of herb chantilly on each portion and serve at once.

Serves 4-6.

PISTOU

75 ml (2½ fl oz/⅓ cup) olive oil
1 onion, chopped
1 small potato, diced
2 carrots, sliced
2 sticks celery, finely sliced
bouquet garni
185 g (6 oz) French beans, cut into short lengths
2 small courgettes (zucchini), sliced
30 g (1 oz) broken spaghetti or pasta shapes
salt and pepper

PISTOU: 3 cloves garlic
4 tablespoons choppped fresh basil
60 g (2 oz/½ cup) freshly grated Parmesan cheese
2 tomatoes, skinned, seeded and chopped

Heat 3 teaspoons oil in a large saucepan, add onion and cook until just beginning to colour. Pour in 1.2 litres (2 pints/5 cups) water and bring to the boil. Add potato, carrots, celery and bouquet garni, and simmer for 10 minutes. Add beans, courgettes (zucchini) and pasta and simmer, uncovered, for 10-15 minutes, until tender.

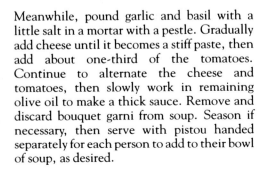

Meanwhile, pound garlic and basil with a little salt in a mortar with a pestle. Gradually add cheese until it becomes a stiff paste, then add about one-third of the tomatoes. Continue to alternate the cheese and tomatoes, then slowly work in remaining olive oil to make a thick sauce. Remove and discard bouquet garni from soup. Season if necessary, then serve with pistou handed separately for each person to add to their bowl of soup, as desired.

Serves 4-6.

CREAM OF BROCCOLI SOUP

30 g (1 oz/6 teaspoons) butter
2 shallots, finely chopped
500 g (1 lb) broccoli flowerets, chopped
1 large potato, diced
1 clove garlic, crushed
500 ml (16 fl oz/2 cups) vegetable stock
500 ml (16 fl oz/2 cups) milk
salt and pepper
pinch grated nutmeg

TO GARNISH: 155 ml (5 fl oz/⅔ cup) single (light) cream
15 g (½ oz/2 tablespoons) ground almonds
¼ teaspoon powdered saffron

Melt butter in a large saucepan, add shallots and cook for 2-3 minutes, until soft. Add broccoli, potato and garlic, cover and cook gently for 5 minutes. Add stock and bring to the boil, then cover and simmer for 20 minutes, until vegetables are tender. Purée in a blender or food processor, then return soup to pan and add milk and salt and pepper and nutmeg. Reheat gently.

To garnish, divide cream between 2 bowls. Mix ground almonds into one and saffron into the other. Ladle soup into individual bowls and place alternate swirls of cream mixtures on top of each.

Serves 4.

CHEESE & ONION PASTRIES

180 g (6 oz / 1½ cups) plain flour
½ teaspoon salt
125 ml (4 fl oz / ½ cup) cold water
24 spring onions
30 g (1 oz) butter
good pinch of cayenne pepper
125 g (4 oz) Gouda cheese, cut into 24 cubes
1 egg, beaten
vegetable oil for deep-frying

Sift the flour with the salt, then add the water to make a firm dough. Knead for 5 minutes, until smooth. Wrap and leave to rest for 30 minutes.

Chop the spring onions, including most of the green tops; there should be about 250 g (8 oz / 1 cup). Gently sauté onions in the butter until softened. Remove from the heat and add the cayenne pepper. Shape the dough into 24 balls and roll each out into a circle about 10 cm (4 in) wide.

Spoon a little spring onion mixture on to each pastry circle, top with a cheese cube and brush edges with the beaten egg. Fold pastry over the filling. Press edges together with a fork to seal. Deep-fry the pastries, a few at a time, in hot oil until golden. Drain and serve warm.

Makes 24.

BLUE CHEESE MUSHROOMS

12 to 14 button mushrooms
125 g (4 oz) blue cheese
125 g (4 oz) full fat soft (cream) cheese
1 tablespoon single cream
pecan nuts and fresh basil or parsley sprigs, to
    garnish

Wipe the mushroom with a clean cloth dipped in cold water to which a few slices of lemon or a few drops of white vinegar has been added.

Cut out the stalks from the mushrooms (They can be used for cooking). Soften the cheeses and beat together until smooth, then beat in the cream. Put into a piping bag fitted with a star nozzle. If preparing ahead, place the mushrooms, covered, and the bag with the filling, in the refrigerator until just before serving.

Pipe the cheese mixture into the mushrooms. Top each with a nut and a basil or parsley sprig. *Makes 12 to 14.*

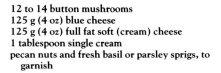

ALMOND CHEESE BALLS

250 g (8 oz / 2 cups) grated mature Cheddar cheese
4 tablespoons plain flour
2 egg whites
180 g (6 oz / 1 cup) blanched almonds
vegetable oil for deep-frying

Combine the cheese and the flour. Beat the egg whites until they form stiff peaks.

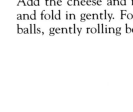

Add the cheese and flour to the egg whites and fold in gently. Form into 16 to 18 small balls, gently rolling between your fingers.

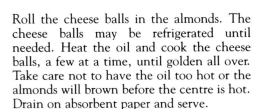

Roll the cheese balls in the almonds. The cheese balls may be refrigerated until needed. Heat the oil and cook the cheese balls, a few at a time, until golden all over. Take care not to have the oil too hot or the almonds will brown before the centre is hot. Drain on absorbent paper and serve.

Makes 16 to 18.

SESAME CHEESE BALLS

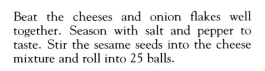

60 g (2 oz) sesame seeds
60 g (2 oz) pepitas or slivered almonds
250 g (8 oz) full fat soft (cream) cheese
2 tablespoons grated Parmesan cheese
2 teaspoons dried onion flakes
salt and pepper

Stir the sesame seeds in a dry frying pan over a moderate heat until they turn golden. Remove to a plate to cool. Put the pepitas or almonds on a baking tray and roast at 180C (350F/Gas 4) for 10 minutes. Cool.

Beat the cheeses and onion flakes well together. Season with salt and pepper to taste. Stir the sesame seeds into the cheese mixture and roll into 25 balls.

Place the toasted pepitas on a sheet of greaseproof paper and roll the cheese balls in the pepitas. Store in the refrigerator or a cool place until ready to serve.

Makes 25.

POTTED CHEESE

250 g (8 oz) Cheddar cheese
60 g (2 oz) blue cheese
30 g (1 oz) butter
2 tablespoons dry sherry
½ teaspoon Worcestershire sauce
¼ teaspoon hot English mustard
1 tablespoon finely chopped fresh herbs
Melba toast or biscuits (crackers), to serve

Grate the Cheddar cheese into a bowl. Add the blue cheese, mixing together with a fork.

Soften the butter and add to the cheese. Blend together well. Gradually beat in the sherry, Worcestershire sauce, mustard and herbs. Blend in a food processor until smooth and thoroughly mixed.

Pack into a serving bowl, cover and chill. The flavours of the cheese improve if it is made 1 or 2 days in advance. Allow the cheese to come to room temperature before serving. Accompany with Melba toast or biscuits (crackers).

Serves 6 to 8.

CHEESE-FILO PASTRIES

500 g (1 lb) feta cheese
3 tablespoons chopped fresh parsley
pepper
3 eggs, beaten
8 sheets filo pastry
125 g (4 oz) butter, melted

Crumble the cheese into a bowl. Mix together the parsley, pepper and beaten eggs. Stir into the cheese and mix together well.

Take 1 sheet of pastry and cut in half, keeping the remainder of the pastry covered with damp absorbent paper to prevent it drying out. Brush the pastry with melted butter and fold into quarters. Put a spoonful of the filling in the centre of each.

Squeeze the pastry around the filling to resemble a money bag (they may be cooked in buttered patty cake tins). Brush pastry with any remaining butter. Bake at 200C (400F/Gas 6) for 20 to 25 minutes, until golden. Serve hot.

Makes 16.

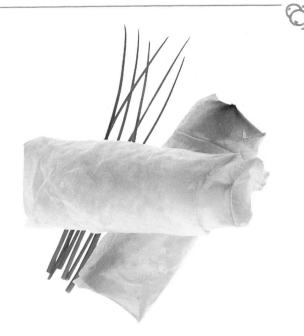

DEEP-FRIED CAMEMBERT

SPINACH & FETA ROLLS

125 g (4 oz) round or semi-circle Camembert cheese, well chilled
1 egg, beaten
60 g (2 oz/½ cup) dry breadcrumbs
125 g (4 oz/¾ cup) sesame seeds
vegetable oil for deep-frying
fresh strawberries, to serve (optional)

Cut the Camembert into 6 wedges.

2 tablespoons vegetable oil
2 onions, finely chopped
250 g (8 oz) packet frozen spinach, defrosted and drained
2 teaspoons dried dill
125 g (4 oz) feta cheese, crumbled
1 egg, beaten
3 tablespoons thick sour cream
12 sheets filo pastry
125 g (4 oz) butter, melted

Gently heat oil in a saucepan and sauté the onions until tender, but not coloured. Add the spinach and sauté for a further 2 minutes. Add the dill and feta cheese.

Dip the wedges of cheese, one at a time, into the beaten egg, turning to coat each wedge. Mix the breadcrumbs and sesame seeds together on a sheet of greaseproof paper.

Remove from the heat and allow to cool. Mix in the egg and sour cream. Chill. Take 1 sheet of the filo pastry, (keep remaining sheets covered with damp absorbent paper) and brush with butter. Top with another sheet of filo and cut into 3 strips.

As each cheese wedge is coated with egg, place in the sesame and breadcrumb mixture, and coat the cheese evenly. If not serving immediately, put on a plate and chill. Heat oil for deep-frying and fry the cheese wedges a few at a time until golden on all sides. Garnish with strawberries and serve.

Makes 6 wedges.

Spoon 1 tablespoon of the spinach mixture on one end of a strip and roll up, tucking in the edges. Brush the end with more butter to seal. Repeat with the remaining pastry and spinach filling. Place the rolls joined end down on baking trays and bake at 200C (400F/Gas 6) for about 15 minutes. Serve hot.

Makes 18.

PEANUT SAUCE & CRUDITÉS

AIOLI & CRUDITÉS

2 cloves garlic
2 tablespoons dark soy sauce
4 tablespoons smooth peanut butter
1 tablespoon sugar
250 ml (8 fl oz/1 cup) water
2 red chillies
selection of crisp vegetables, such as carrots, celery, a cucumber, radishes and a cauliflower

Crush the garlic and place in a small saucepan with the soy sauce, peanut butter, sugar and water.

4 cloves garlic
½ teaspoon salt
2 egg yolks
250 ml (8 fl oz/1 cup) virgin olive oil
juice of ½ lemon
crisp vegetables, such as carrots, celery and radish, to serve

Crush the garlic into a bowl, add the salt and egg yolks. Whisk together well. Add 1 or 2 drops of oil and whisk.

Shred the chillies, removing the seeds. Put the chilli shreds into the pan and heat together. Simmer for 5 minutes, stirring constantly. If the mixture is very thin, simmer until it thickens slightly. Leave to cool. The sauce sometimes becomes solid when cool. When this happens thin with a little water. Pour into a serving bowl.

Continue whisking the egg yolk mixture, gradually adding the oil until about 2 tablespoons of the oil has been added. Add the remaining oil in a fine stream, whisking all the time. If the mixture becomes too thick, add a little hot water. Add the lemon juice and season with more salt, if needed. Cover and refrigerate.

Prepare the vegetables for dipping. Cut carrots, celery and cucumber into 10 cm (4 in) fingers. Remove stems and roots from radishes. Break the cauliflower into florets – they may be blanched in boiling water if preferred. To serve, surround the bowl of dipping sauce with the vegetables.

Serves 4 to 6.

Peel carrot and cut into 10 cm (4 in) lengths. Cut celery the same size and trim stem and root from radishes. Pile around the Aioli on a large platter. The vegetables are dipped into the Aioli before eating. Other vegetables such as mange tout (snow peas), cucumber sticks, fresh cauliflower florets, blanched asparagus tips and spring onions go well.

Serves 6 to 8.

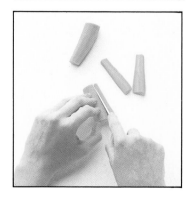

MARINATED ARTICHOKES

MEXICAN BEAN DIP

400 g (14 oz) can artichoke hearts
6 tablespoons olive or vegetable oil
pepper
3 tablespoons chopped fresh mixed herbs
salt
juice of ½ lemon
red chilli slivers (optional)
1 clove garlic, crushed (optional)

Drain the artichokes and rinse well under a cold running water to remove all the brine. Drain again and cut into halves or quarters.

Place the artichokes in a bowl, add the oil, a good grinding of pepper and the herbs. Mix together well, cover and refrigerate until ready to serve. Toss again before serving and add a squeeze of lemon juice and salt to taste.

For a bite, some slivers of fresh red chilli may be added to the artichokes; for garlic lovers, add a crushed garlic clove before chilling. The artichokes may be stored in a jar for up to 2 weeks, provided they are covered with the oil. Serve at room temperature. They may also be served on a croûton or added to salads.

Serves 4 to 6.

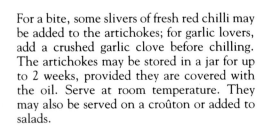

465 g (15 oz) canned red kidney beans
2 tablespoons vegetable oil
90 g (3 oz/¾ cup) grated Cheddar cheese
½ teaspoon salt
1 teaspoon chilli powder
1 tablespoon chopped green pepper (capsicum)
corn chips or prawn crisps for dipping

Drain the beans, reserving the liquid for the dip.

Heat the oil in a small pan and add the beans, mashing with a potato masher as they cook. Add 3 tablespoons of the reserved bean liquid and stir in until well mixed. Cool. Add cheese, salt and chilli powder. If the mixture is thick, add more of the reserved bean liquid until it is a good consistency for scooping. Add the pepper. Serve hot with corn chips or prawn crisps.

Serves 4 to 6.

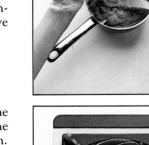

If using prawn crisps, drop a few at a time into deep hot oil. When they come to the top, remove almost immediately and drain. The crisps take only a few seconds to cook. Drain on absorbent paper and store in an airtight container until ready to use.

ASPARAGUS ROLLS

25 spears fresh or canned asparagus
4 egg yolks
250 g (8 oz) butter
squeeze of lemon juice
1 tablespoon chopped fresh mint
1 loaf unsliced bread

If using fresh asparagus, trim the stalks and cook in a pan of boiling water for 8 minutes. Drain and rinse with cold water. If using canned asparagus, drain.

To make the Hollandaise sauce, whip the egg yolks in a food processor until frothy. Melt the butter. When very hot, gradually add to the yolks, in a thin stream, with the processor on all the time. Transfer to a bowl and chill the mixture until thickened. Flavour the Hollandaise with lemon juice to taste and stir in the mint.

Use a serrated or electric knife to cut the bread into 25 thin slices. Cut away the crusts. Spread bread slices with the Hollandaise sauce and place one asparagus spear, cut in half, on each piece. Join two corners of each with a wooden toothpick. Dot with more sauce. Place under a preheated grill and cook until crispy.

Makes 25.

MARINATED MUSHROOMS

500 g (1 lb) button mushrooms
250 ml (8 fl oz/1 cup) water
2 teaspoons salt
125 ml (4 fl oz/½ cup) white wine vinegar
1 bay leaf
few sprigs fresh thyme
1 clove garlic
2 tablespoons olive oil
1 lemon
finely chopped parsley

Trim mushroom stalks. If necessary, wipe the mushrooms with a cloth dipped in water with a little lemon juice added.

Boil the water with the salt, vinegar, bay leaf, thyme, garlic and the oil. Put the mushrooms in a heatproof bowl and pour the boiling mixture over. When cool, refrigerate for at least 12 hours, or up to 3 days.

Drain the mushrooms and put in a serving bowl. Using a citrus zester, cut the lemon rind into fine strips and sprinkle over the mushrooms with the chopped parsley.

Serves 6 to 8.

MUSHROOM PASTIES

DOLMADES

125 g (4 oz/1 cup) plain flour
90 g (3 oz) butter
1 tablespoon water
3 spring onions, chopped
250 g (8 oz) button mushrooms, chopped
1 tablespoon plain flour
1 tablespoon dry sherry
¼ teaspoon dry mustard
2 tablespoons milk
8 olives, sliced
salt and pepper
1 egg beaten, to glaze

Sift flour into a bowl and rub in 60 g (2 oz) butter. Add the water to make a firm dough. Wrap and chill.

Sauté the onions in the remaining butter in a frying pan, without browning. Add the mushrooms and cook, stirring, until all the liquid evaporates. Stir in the flour and mix well. Add the sherry, mustard and milk and stir until mixture boils. Add the olives and season to taste. Allow this mushroom filling to cool.

Thinly roll out the pastry on a floured surface and cut into 7.5 cm (3 in) rounds. Brush edges with egg. Put a good teaspoonful of the filling in the centre of each round. Bring up the edges to join and pinch together. Place on greased baking trays, brush with egg to glaze and bake at 200C (400F/Gas 6) for 15 to 20 minutes.

Makes 10.

180 g (6 oz) packet vine leaves
1 onion, finely chopped
2 tablespoons olive oil
500 g (16 oz/2 cups) cooked rice
salt and pepper
2 tablespoons chopped fresh mint
90 g (3 oz/1 cup) toasted pine nuts

Drain the vine leaves, rinse well and soak in cold water to remove the brine, separating the leaves carefully. Drain.

Gently sauté the onion in the oil. When tender, add to the rice and season to taste with salt and pepper. Stir in the mint and half the nuts. Place 2 teaspoons of this filling on each vine leaf, roll up and tuck in the edges.

Pack stuffed vine leaves close together in a shallow pan, making more than 1 layer if necessary, and separating the layers with extra vine leaves. Add enough hot water barely to cover the vine leaves. Place a plate directly on top of the rolls with a can on top to weigh them down. Cover and simmer for 30 minutes. Cool, then chill. Serve garnished with remaining pine nuts.

Makes about 45.

FETA CHEESE KEBABS

220 g (7 oz) feta cheese
¼ red pepper (capsicum)
¼ yellow pepper (capsicum)
1 courgette (zucchini)
¼ aubergine (eggplant)
thyme sprigs, to garnish

MARINADE: 6 teaspoons olive oil
3 teaspoons raspberry vinegar
1 teaspoon pink peppercorns, crushed
1 teaspoon clear honey
½ teaspoon Dijon mustard
2 teaspoons chopped fresh thyme
¼ teaspoon salt
½ teaspoon ground black pepper

To make marinade, place oil, vinegar, peppercorns, honey, mustard, thyme, salt and pepper in a large bowl. Stir mixture together with a wooden spoon until thoroughly blended. Cut feta cheese, peppers (capsicums), courgette (zucchini) and aubergine (eggplant) into bite-sized pieces. Add to marinade, stir well to coat evenly, cover with plastic wrap and leave in a cool place for at least 1 hour.

Thread one piece of each ingredient onto wooden cocktail sticks. Just before serving, cook under a hot grill for 2-3 minutes until vegetables are just tender. Arrange on a serving plate, garnished with sprigs of thyme.

Makes 24.

MOZZARELLA SALAD

185 g (6 oz) Mozzarella cheese
2 large beefsteak tomatoes
2 ripe avocados
2 shallots
90 ml (3 fl oz/⅓ cup) olive oil
2 tablespoons lemon juice
½ teaspoon caster sugar
¼-½ teaspoon dry mustard
1-2 teaspoons green peppercorns, crushed
½ teaspoon dried oregano
salt
sprig of basil, to garnish
crusty bread or bread sticks, to serve

Thinly slice Mozzarella cheese and tomatoes and arrange on 4 small plates.

Cut avocados in half, remove stones and peel. Cut avocados into neat slices and arrange on plate. Peel and thinly slice shallots, separate into rings and scatter over salad.

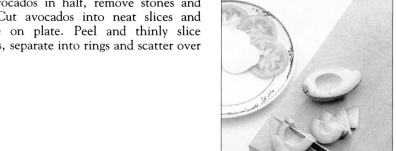

Put remaining ingredients, except basil and bread, into a screw-topped jar, adding salt to taste, and shake vigorously until well blended. Spoon over salad and leave to marinate for 1 hour before serving. Serve chilled, garnished with basil, with warm crusty bread or bread sticks.

Serves 4.

VEGETABLE CURRY ENVELOPES

— MUSHROOMS & GRAPEFRUIT —

60 g (2 oz) puff pastry, thawed
1 egg, beaten
1 teaspoon cumin seeds

FILLING: 15 g (½ oz/3 teaspoons) butter
1 leek, finely chopped
1 clove garlic, crushed
1 teaspoon ground cumin
1 teaspoon garam masala
2 teaspoons mango chutney
½ teaspoon finely grated lime peel
2 teaspoons lime juice
60 g (2 oz) cooked, diced potato

250 g (8 oz) button mushrooms
fresh mint leaves or chives, to garnish

MARINADE: 1 large pink grapefruit
90 ml (3 fl oz/⅓ cup) ginger wine
2 teaspoons mint jelly
½ teaspoon salt
½ teaspoon ground black pepper
1 teaspoon Dijon mustard

Melt butter for filling in a small saucepan.
Add leek and garlic to pan.

To make marinade, cut away grapefruit peel
and white pith from flesh, allowing juice to
fall into a small saucepan. Cut out segments
between membranes and place on a plate.

Cook quickly for 1 minute, stirring. Add
cumin, garam masala, chutney, lime peel and
juice. Stir well, cook gently for 1-2 minutes,
then add potatoes, mix well and cool.
Preheat oven to 220C (425F/Gas 7). Roll out
puff pastry very thinly to an oblong measuring
30 × 20 cm (12 × 8 in). Cut into twenty-four
5 cm (2 in) squares. Brush edges with beaten
egg and place a little filling in centre of each.

Squeeze remaining juice from membranes
into saucepan. Add ginger wine, mint jelly,
salt, pepper and mustard; bring to the boil
and stir in mushrooms. Pour into a bowl and
leave until cold.

Draw all corners to centre and seal joins to
form a tiny envelope. Repeat to seal all pastry
envelopes. Arrange on a baking sheet, brush
with egg to glaze and sprinkle with cumin
seeds. Cook in the oven for 5-8 minutes until
well risen and golden brown.

Makes 24.

Cut grapefruit segments into bite-sized
pieces. Thread 2 mushrooms and a piece of
grapefruit onto each cocktail stick and
garnish with mint leaves or chives.

Makes 24.

PESTO SAUCE

30 g (1 oz/1¼ cups) fresh basil leaves, tightly packed
2 garlic cloves
Coarse or rock salt
2 tablespoons pine nuts
125 ml (4 fl oz/½ cup) olive oil
2 tablespoons freshly grated Parmesan cheese
2 tablespoons freshly grated pecorino cheese, or additional 2 tablespoons freshly grated Parmesan

Place basil, garlic, salt and pine nuts in a blender or food processor. Whirl until finely chopped.

With motor running, add oil in a thin stream. Scrape down sides to make sure all solids are well mixed. Continue blending to make a smooth sauce.

Add cheeses and give the machine one short burst to blend ingredients well. Serve hot over freshly-cooked pasta.

Makes about 500 ml (16 fl oz/2 cups).

Note: Use only a high-quality olive oil and do not substitute vegetable or peanut oil. If the sauce is too thick, thin with a little of the pasta cooking water. Store any leftover sauce in a sealed container in the refrigerator for up to 1 month.

TOMATO SAUCE

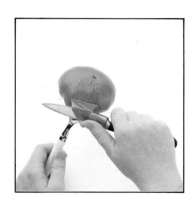

1 kg (2 lb) ripe tomatoes
1½ tablespoons olive oil
125 g (4 oz) onion, finely chopped
1 celery stalk, finely chopped
2 tablespoons tomato purée (paste)
1 bay leaf
6 fresh basil leaves, or 1 teaspoon dried basil
1 teaspoon sugar
1 teaspoon salt
Pepper

Dip tomatoes in boiling water to split the skin, then spear with a fork and skin. Quarter tomatoes and set aside.

In a heavy-based saucepan, heat oil over a low heat. Sauté onions and celery until onions are golden. Add tomatoes and any juice, tomato purée (paste), bay leaf, basil, sugar, and salt and pepper.

Bring to the boil. Lower heat and simmer gently, uncovered, for 45 minutes, stirring occasionally. Remove bay leaf and discard. Serve hot with freshly-cooked pasta.

Makes about 600 ml (20 fl oz/2½ cups).

CARIBBEAN CREOLE SAUCE

125 ml (4 fl oz/½ cup) vegetable oil
2 medium onions, chopped
1 medium green pepper (capsicum), cored, seeded and finely chopped
2 garlic cloves
1 teaspoon finely chopped, seeded fresh red chilli
1 teaspoon salt
pepper
3 tomatoes, skinned and chopped
180 g (6 oz) tomato purée (paste)
125 ml (4 fl oz/½ cup) dry white wine

In a heavy-based saucepan, heat oil over moderate heat. Add onions, green pepper (capsicum), garlic and chilli; sauté until the peppers are soft.

Add salt and pepper and tomatoes. Cook about 10 minutes over low heat, stirring occasionally.

Add tomato purée (paste) and wine and simmer, stirring occasionally. Serve the piquant sauce hot with boiled rice.

Makes about 500 ml (16 fl oz/2 cups).

MARINARA SAUCE

1 to 2 small fresh red chillies, according to taste
12 large black olives, stoned and chopped
1 tablespoon capers, drained
125 ml (4 fl oz/½ cup) olive oil
1 medium onion, finely chopped
2 garlic cloves, finely chopped
2 teaspoons chopped fresh oregano or ½ teaspoon dried oregano
500 g (1 lb) ripe tomatoes or 500 g (1 lb) canned skinned tomatoes

Slice each chilli and use the tip of a knife to remove seeds.

In a glass or ceramic bowl, marinate the olives, chillies and capers in 4 tablespoons oil for at least 1 hour. Meanwhile, gently sauté the onion and garlic in the remaining oil until golden. Add the oregano.

Skin fresh tomatoes; use a spoon to scoop out seeds, then chop. Strain canned tomatoes. Turn all ingredients into a flame-proof casserole or large frying pan and cook over moderate to high heat until the mixture thickens and darkens slightly. Remove chillies. Serve the sauce hot with pasta.

Makes about 500 ml (16 fl oz/2 cups).

TAMIL NADU VEGETABLES

PEPPERS WITH CAULIFLOWER

125 g (4 oz/²/₃ cup) red split lentils
½ teaspoon turmeric
1 small aubergine (eggplant)
60 ml (2 fl oz/¼ cup) vegetable oil
30 g (1 oz/¹/₃ cup) desiccated coconut
1 teaspoon cumin seeds
½ teaspoon mustard seeds
2 dried red chillies, crushed
1 red pepper (capsicum), seeded and sliced
125 g (4 oz) courgettes (zucchini), thickly sliced
90 g (3 oz) green beans, cut into 2 cm (¾ in) pieces
155 ml (5 fl oz/²/₃ cup) vegetable stock
salt
red pepper (capsicum) strips, to garnish

60 ml (2 fl oz/¼ cup) vegetable oil
1 large onion, sliced
2 cloves garlic, crushed
2 green chillies, seeded and chopped
1 cauliflower, cut into small flowerets
½ teaspoon turmeric
1 teaspoon Garam Masala
1 green pepper (capsicum)
1 red pepper (capsicum)
1 orange or yellow pepper (capsicum)
salt and pepper
1 tablespoon chopped fresh coriander, to garnish

Wash lentils and put in a large saucepan with turmeric and 625 ml (20 fl oz/2½ cups) water. Bring to the boil, then reduce heat and simmer, covered, for 15-20 minutes, until lentils are soft. Meanwhile, cut aubergine (eggplant) into 1 cm (½ in) dice. Heat oil in a large shallow pan, add coconut, cumin and mustard seeds and chillies.

Heat oil in a large saucepan, add onion and fry over a medium heat for 8 minutes or until soft and golden brown. Stir in garlic, chillies and cauliflower and fry for 5 minutes, stirring occasionally. Stir in turmeric and garam masala and fry for 1 minute.

Fry for 1 minute, then add aubergine (egg-plant), red pepper (capsicum), courgettes (zucchini), green beans, stock and salt. Bring to the boil, then simmer, covered, for 10-15 minutes, until the vegetables are just tender. Stir in lentils and any cooking liquid and cook for a further 5 minutes. Serve hot, garnished with red pepper (capsicum) strips.

Serves 4.

Reduce heat, add 60 ml (2 fl oz/¼ cup) water and cook, covered, for 10-15 minutes, until cauliflower is almost tender. Cut peppers (capsicums) in half lengthwise, remove stalks and seeds, then slice peppers (capsicums) finely. Add to pan and cook for a further 3-5 minutes, until softened. Season with salt and pepper. Serve hot, garnished with chopped coriander.

Serves 4.

MUSHROOM CURRY

DHAL

500 g (1 lb) button mushrooms
2 fresh green chillies, seeded
2 teaspoons ground coriander
1 teaspoon ground cumin
½ teaspoon chilli powder
2 cloves garlic, crushed
1 onion, cut into wedges
155 ml (5 fl oz/⅔ cup) coconut milk
salt
30 g (1 oz/6 teaspoons) butter or ghee
bay leaves, to garnish

Wipe mushrooms and trim stalks, then set aside.

250 g (8 oz/1¼ cups) brown lentils
1 teaspoon turmeric
1 clove garlic, crushed
30 g (1 oz/6 teaspoons) ghee
1 large onion, chopped
1 teaspoon Garam Masala
½ teaspoon ground ginger
1 teaspoon ground coriander
½ teaspoon cayenne pepper
coriander leaves, to garnish

Wash lentils in cold water.

Put chillies, ground coriander, cumin, chilli powder, garlic, onion, coconut milk and salt to taste in a blender or food processor fitted with a metal blade and blend until smooth.

Place lentils in a saucepan with 940 ml (30 fl oz/3¾ cups) water, turmeric and garlic. Stir well, then cover and simmer for 30 minutes until tender. Uncover and cook for 2-3 minutes to reduce excess liquid.

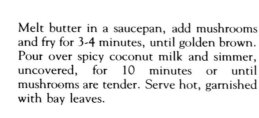

Melt butter in a saucepan, add mushrooms and fry for 3-4 minutes, until golden brown. Pour over spicy coconut milk and simmer, uncovered, for 10 minutes or until mushrooms are tender. Serve hot, garnished with bay leaves.

Serves 4.

Heat ghee in a pan. Add onion and fry gently for 5 minutes, then add garam masala, ginger, coriander and cayenne and cook gently for 1 minute. Add mixture to lentils and stir well. Serve hot, garnished with coriander leaves.

Serves 4-6.

Note: for a less fiery flavour, reduce cayenne pepper.

VEGETABLE COUSCOUS

250 g (8 oz) couscous
4 tablespoons olive oil
2 onions, coarsely chopped
1 large aubergine (eggplant), diced
500 g (1 lb) acorn squash, seeded and diced
2 carrots, sliced
1 teaspoon Harissa
2 tomatoes, skinned and chopped
2 tablespoons tomato purée (paste)
470 ml (15 fl oz/2 cups) vegetable stock
410 g (13 oz) can chick peas, drained
2 courgettes (zucchini), sliced
60 g (2 oz/⅓ cup) sultanas or raisins
2 teaspoons chopped fresh parsley
sprig of coriander or parsley, to garnish

Put couscous in a bowl with 470 ml (15 fl oz/2 cups) water. Leave to soak for 15 minutes until water is absorbed. Heat oil in a saucepan. Add onions, aubergine (egg plant), squash and carrots and fry for 5 minutes, stirring frequently. Stir in harissa, tomatoes, tomato purée (paste) and stock. Bring to the boil and stir well. Line a large metal sieve or colander with muslin or all-purpose kitchen cloth and place over pan.

Put couscous into sieve. Cover whole pan with foil to enclose steam, then simmer for 20 minutes. Add chick peas, courgettes (zucchini) and sultanas or raisins to pan, stir well, then replace sieve and fluff up couscous with a fork. Cover again with foil and simmer for a further 20 minutes. Spread couscous on a large serving dish and fluff up with a fork. Add parsley to mixture in pan and spoon mixture over couscous. Serve hot, garnished with sprig of coriander or parsley.

Serves 4-6.

VEGETARIAN MEDLEY

125 g (4 oz/¾ cup) whole green lentils
125 g (4 oz/¾ cup) split peas
2 leeks, cut into 0.5 cm (¼ in) slices
2 courgettes (zucchini), cut into 0.5 cm (¼ in) slices
2 carrots, thinly sliced
2 sticks celery, thinly sliced
1 onion, coarsely chopped
1 clove garlic, crushed
30 g (1 oz/6 teaspoons) ghee
½ teaspoon turmeric
1 teaspoon mustard seeds
2 teaspoons Garam Masala
salt
celery leaves and slices of lemon, to garnish

Soak lentils and split peas overnight. Drain lentils and peas and put into a saucepan. Add 625 ml (20 fl oz/2½ cups) cold water, bring to the boil and boil for 10 minutes. Add vegetables and garlic to pan, then cover and cook gently for 10 minutes.

Meanwhile, melt ghee in a pan. Add turmeric, mustard seeds and garam masala and cook gently for 2 minutes until seeds begin to pop. Stir into lentil mixture and continue cooking for a further 15 minutes or until vegetables and lentils are tender and liquid has been absorbed. Season with salt, garnish with celery leaves and slices of lemon and serve hot.

Serves 4.

125 g (4 oz / 1 cup) plain flour
pinch of salt
2 eggs
315 ml (10 fl oz / 1¼ cups) milk
3 teaspoons butter, melted
vegetable oil for cooking
TO SERVE: lemon juice and sugar, or
warmed jam

Sift flour and salt into a bowl. Make a well in centre and add eggs and a little milk. Beat, working in all flour. Beat in remaining milk and butter.

Heat a little vegetable oil in a 17.5 cm (7 in) crêpe pan, barely covering the base. Pour in 2–3 tablespoons batter, tilting the pan so the batter covers the base thinly and evenly. Cook over high heat for about 1 minute, until lightly browned underneath.

Turn crêpe with a palette knife and cook other side for about 30 seconds. Remove from pan and keep warm, then continue until all the batter is used.

Makes 8.

WHOLEMEAL CRÊPES

125 g (4 oz / 1 cup) plain wholemeal flour
½ teaspoon salt
3 eggs
315 ml (10 fl oz / 1¼ cups) milk
vegetable oil for cooking

Stir flour and salt into a bowl. Make a well in the centre and add the eggs and a little of the milk. Beat well with a wooden spoon, working in all the flour, then gradually beat in the remaining milk until the batter is bubbling.

Heat a little vegetable oil in a 17.5 cm (7 in) crêpe pan, barely covering the base. Pour in 2–3 tablespoons batter, tilting the pan so the batter covers the base thinly and evenly. Cook over high heat for about 1 minute, until lightly browned underneath.

Turn crêpe with a palette knife and cook other side for about 30 seconds. Remove from pan and keep warm, then continue until all the batter is used.

Makes 8.

MOZZARELLA CRÊPES

eight 17.5 (7 in) crêpes, see page 32
60 g (2 oz / ¼ cup) butter
2.5 cm (1 in) thick slice bread, cubed
100g (4 oz) diced Mozzarella cheese
salt and pepper
30g (1 oz / ¼ cup) grated Parmesan cheese
fresh basil sprigs, to garnish

Keep crêpes warm while preparing filling. Heat butter in a frying pan and fry the bread cubes until golden on all sides. Remove from heat, stir in cheese and season to taste with salt and pepper.

Divide filling between crêpes and roll up. Put in a single layer in a shallow flameproof serving dish, sprinkle with Parmesan cheese and brown under a hot grill for 2 minutes, until the Parmesan is light golden and bubbling. Garnish with basil sprigs and serve.

Serves 4.

PARMESAN CRÊPES

eight 17.5 cm (7 in) crêpes, see page 32
2 tablespoons vegetable oil
30 g (1 oz / 6 teaspoons) butter
250g (8 oz) potatoes, cooked and diced
salt and pepper
60g (2 oz / 1 cup) fresh breadcrumbs
60 g (2 oz / ¼ cup) butter, melted
3 teaspoons chopped fresh parsley
60g (2 oz / ½ cup) Parmesan cheese
fresh parsley sprigs, to garnish

Keep crêpes warm while preparing filling. Heat oil and butter in a frying pan and cook potatoes until crisp and golden. Drain well on absorbent kitchen paper, then season to taste with salt and pepper.

Divide potato cubes between crêpes and fold into quarters. Put in a single layer in a shallow flameproof serving dish. Mix together breadcrumbs, melted butter and chopped parsley, then sprinkle over crêpes with Parmesan cheese. Put under a medium grill for 4–5 minutes, until crisp and golden. Garnish with fresh parsley sprigs and serve at once.

Serves 4.

ASPARAGUS CRÊPES

eight 17.5 cm (7 in) crêpes, see page 32
375 g (12 oz) fresh or canned asparagus tips
30 g (1 oz/6 teaspoons) butter
2 teaspoons plain flour
155 ml (5 fl oz/⅔ cup) single (light) cream
1 teaspoon chopped fresh parsley
1 teaspoon chopped fresh chives
salt and pepper
1 tablespoon grated Parmesan cheese

Keep crêpes warm while preparing filling. If asparagus is fresh, cook in boiling salted water for 6 minutes, then drain well. If canned, drain well.

Melt butter into a saucepan over low heat, then stir in flour and cook for 30 seconds. Stir in cream and continue cooking gently until thick, then stir in parsley and chives and season to taste with salt and pepper.

Stir asparagus tips into sauce. Divide filling between crêpes and roll up. Put in a single layer in a shallow flameproof serving dish, sprinkle with Parmesan cheese and brown under a hot grill for 2 minutes, until the Parmesan is light golden and bubbling.

Serves 4.

Note: Garnish with extra asparagus tips, if desired.

SWEETCORN LAYERS

eight 17.5 cm (7 in) crêpes, see page 32
1 onion, finely chopped
30 g (1 oz/6 teaspoons) butter
440 g (14 oz) can sweetcorn kernels, drained
315 ml (10 fl oz/1¼ cups) cheese sauce
1 teaspoon chopped fresh marjoram
30 g (1 oz/¼ cup) grated Cheddar cheese
fresh marjoram sprigs, to garnish

Keep crêpes warm while preparing filling. Put onion and butter into a saucepan and cook over low heat for 5 minutes, until soft, then stir in sweetcorn kernels and heat through.

Reserve 6 tablespoons cheese sauce and mix the remainder with the corn, then add the marjoram.

Put one crêpe on a large flame-proof serving plate and spread with some of the corn mixture. Top with a second crêpe and repeat until all the crêpes and corn mixture are used, finishing with a crêpe.

Spread reserved cheese sauce on top and sprinkle with grated cheese. Brown under a hot grill for 3 minutes, until sauce is bubbling. Garnish with fresh marjoram and serve at once, cut into wedges.

Serves 4.

MUSHROOM CRÊPES

eight 17.5 cm (7 in) crêpes, see page 32
60 g (2 oz / ¼ cup) butter
250 g (8 oz) mushrooms, thinly sliced
60 g (2 oz / ½ cup) plain flour
315 ml (10 fl oz / 1¼ cups) milk
¼ teaspoon grated nutmeg
salt and pepper
chopped fresh parsley and sprigs and mushroom slices, to garnish

Keep crêpes warm while preparing filling. Melt butter in a large saucepan, add mushrooms, cover and cook over low heat for 5 minutes.

Stir in the flour and cook for 1 minute, stirring, then gradually add milk, stirring well. Bring to the boil and simmer for 3 minutes. Season with nutmeg and salt and pepper.

Preheat oven to 180C (350F/Gas 4). Divide filling between crêpes. Roll up and put in a single layer in a shallow ovenproof serving dish, cover with foil and heat through in the oven for 20 minutes. Garnish with chopped parsley and sprigs and mushroom slices. Serve hot.

Serves 4.

SPINACH CRÊPES

eight 17.5 cm (7 in) crêpes, see page 32
1 kg (2 lb) fresh spinach, stalks removed
1 onion, finely chopped
30 g (1 oz / 6 teaspoons) butter
3 teaspoons tomato purée (paste)
1 teaspoon paprika
salt and pepper
2 hard-boiled eggs, chopped
30 g (1 oz / ¼ cup) grated Parmesan cheese
fresh parsley sprigs, to garnish

Keep crêpes warm while preparing filling. Wash spinach very well and put into a large saucepan with only the water clinging to its leaves. Cover and heat gently until spinach is cooked and very tender. Drain

well and press out excess moisture, then finely chop and set aside.

Put onion and butter into a large pan and cook over low heat for 5 minutes, until soft. Stir in tomato purée (paste) and paprika and simmer for 2 minutes. Season with salt and pepper and stir in eggs.

Divide spinach between crêpes and spread over surface, then top with egg mixture and roll up. Put in a single layer in a shallow flameproof serving dish, sprinkle with Parmesan cheese and brown under a hot grill for 2 minutes, until the Parmesan is light golden and bubbling. Garnish with parsley sprigs and serve.

Serves 4.

BASIC OMELETTE

3 eggs

salt and pepper

15 g (½ oz/3 teaspoons) butter

watercress sprig and tomato slice, to garnish

In a bowl, beat eggs with salt and pepper to taste until just mixed. Put omelette pan over low heat to become thoroughly hot.

Put butter into pan. When butter is sizzling but not brown, pour in eggs. Using a fork or spatula, draw mixture from sides to middle of pan, allowing uncooked egg to run underneath. Repeat 2 or 3 times so egg is pushed up lightly and becomes fluffy. Cook for about 2 minutes, until golden-brown underneath and the top is still slightly runny.

CURRIED OMELETTE

one 3-egg Basic Omelette

1 onion, finely chopped

30 g (1 oz/6 teaspoons) butter

2 teaspoons curry powder

1 eating apple, peeled, cored and finely diced

3 teaspoons mango chutney, finely chopped

salt and pepper

squeeze of lemon juice

apple slices and fresh coriander sprigs, to garnish

Prepare filling before making omelette. Put onion into a frying pan with butter and cook over low heat for 3 minutes. Stir in curry powder and apple and continue cooking over low heat for 5 minutes, then stir in chutney and season to taste with salt and pepper and lemon juice.

Make omelette and spoon curry mixture over half the egg mixture. Fold omelette over and cut in half to serve. Garnish with a few apple slices and fresh coriander sprigs.

Serves 2.

Using a palette knife, fold over one-third of mixture away from handle. Hold over a warm serving plate, with the palm of your hand uppermost. Shake the omelette to the edge of the pan and tip completely over to make another fold. Garnish with watercress and tomato slice and serve at once.

Serves 1.

ITALIAN OMELETTE

60 g (2 oz/¼ cup) butter
1 small onion, finely chopped
1 tomato, skinned and chopped
1 tablespoon chopped green pepper (capsicum)
3 eggs
60 g (2 oz/⅓ cup) cooked pasta, well drained
salt and pepper
6 teaspoons grated Parmesan cheese
fresh basil sprig, to garnish

Prepare filling before making omelette. Melt half butter in a small saucepan, add onion and cook over low heat for 2 minutes. Stir in tomato and pepper (capsicum), cover and cook over low heat for 10 minutes.

In a bowl, beat eggs and stir in pasta with salt and pepper. Melt remaining butter in a 17.5 cm (7 in) omelette pan. Pour in mixture and cook over low heat, drawing cooked egg from edge of pan towards middle until just set.

Spread filling over half of the omelette and fold over. Sprinkle with cheese and put under hot grill for 30 seconds to melt the cheese. Cut in half, garnish with basil and serve at once.

Serves 1.

FLORENTINE OMELETTE

125 g (4 oz) fresh spinach
155 ml (5 fl oz/⅔ cup) cheese sauce
one 3-egg Basic Omelette, see page 36
60 g (2 oz/½ cup) grated Cheddar cheese
cayenne pepper for sprinkling

Prepare filling before making omelette. Wash the spinach very well, drain and put into a saucepan with only the water clinging to its leaves. Cover and cook over low heat until spinach has shrunk and is very tender. Drain well and press out excess moisture. Set aside. Warm through sauce and keep warm.

Make omelette and fill with spinach. Fold over and lift onto warm flameproof serving plate. Spoon over cheese sauce and sprinkle on the grated cheese. Put under hot grill until sauce is bubbling and golden, sprinkle with cayenne pepper and serve at once.

Serves 1.

— POTATO & HERB OMELETTE —

3 teaspoons vegetable oil
1 large potato, cooked and thinly sliced
1 teaspoon chopped fresh rosemary
1 teaspoon chopped fresh chervil
salt and pepper
one 3-egg Basic Omelette, see page 36
fresh rosemary and chervil sprigs, to garnish

Prepare filling before making omelette. Heat the oil in a frying pan, add the potato slices in a single layer and fry until crisp and golden. Drain well on absorbent kitchen paper.

Mix potatoes with rosemary and chervil and season well with salt and pepper. Keep warm.

Make omelette and put potato mixture on half of the omelette. Fold omelette over, garnish with rosemary and chervil and serve at once.

Serves 1.

— FLUFFY CHEESE OMELETTE —

3 eggs, separated
salt and pepper
15 g (½ oz/3 teaspoons) butter
60 g (2 oz/½ cup) grated Red Leicester cheese or other red cheese
fresh chervil sprigs, to garnish

In a bowl, beat egg yolks with salt and pepper to taste until creamy. Whisk whites to stiff peaks in a separate bowl and fold into yolks. Melt butter in a 17.5 cm (7 in) omelette pan, pour in egg mixture and cook over low heat for 2-3 minutes, until base is set and golden-brown.

Lift omelette on to a warm flameproof plate. Sprinkle three-quarters of the cheese over surface and fold omelette in half, then sprinkle remaining cheese on top. Put under hot grill for 30 seconds, to melt cheese. Garnish with chervil, then serve at once.

Serves 1.

FRIAR'S OMELETTE

60 g (2 oz/¼ cup) butter
2 medium slices white bread, crusts removed and cut into 1 cm (½ in) cubes
2 tomatoes, skinned and chopped
6 eggs
½ teaspoon chopped fresh mixed herbs
salt and pepper
whole chives, to garnish

Preheat oven to 160C (325F/Gas 3). Melt butter in a 20 cm (8 in) omelette pan with an ovenproof handle. Add bread cubes and fry over medium heat, stirring occasionally, until lightly browned all over, then add tomatoes and continue cooking for 1 minute. In a bowl, beat eggs with herbs and salt and pepper to taste.

Pour eggs into pan and cook for 1 minute, moving eggs from edge of pan to centre so liquid egg runs to base of pan.

Transfer to oven and cook for 10 minutes, until set. This omelette is good served hot or cold. Cut into wedges to serve and garnish with whole chives.

Serves 2–3.

COTTAGE CHEESE OMELETTE

4 eggs, separated
250 g (8 oz) cottage cheese
salt and pepper
30 g (1 oz/6 teaspoons) butter
2 tomatoes, skinned and sliced
fresh parsley sprigs, to garnish

Preheat oven to 160C (325F/Gas 3). In a bowl, beat egg yolks lightly, then add cottage cheese and salt and pepper to taste and beat well. In a separate bowl, whisk whites to stiff peaks and fold into egg mixture.

Melt butter in a 20 cm (8 in) omelette pan with an ovenproof handle. Pour in egg mixture, spreading lightly, and cook for 1 minute. Place tomato slices in a single layer on top of omelette, then transfer to oven and cook for 10 minutes, until set. Do not fold this omelette but, instead, serve cut in half. Serve at once, garnished with fresh parsley sprigs.

Serves 2.

— CHEESE SOUFFLÉ OMELETTE —

5 eggs, separated
salt and pepper
30 g (1 oz / 6 teaspoons) butter
6 spring onions, finely chopped
155 ml (5 fl oz / ⅔ cup) cheese sauce
30 g (1 oz / ¼ cup) grated Cheddar cheese
spring onion, to garnish

Preheat oven to 160C (325F/Gas 3). In a bowl, beat egg yolks with salt and pepper to taste. In a separate bowl, whisk whites to stiff peaks and fold into egg mixture.

Melt butter in a 20 cm (8 in) omelette pan with an ovenproof handle. Pour in egg mixture, spreading lightly, and cook for 1 minute.

Sprinkle omelette with onions, then transfer to oven and cook for 5 minutes, until half set. Quickly spoon on cheese sauce and sprinkle with cheese. Return to oven and continue cooking for 5 minutes, until set. Do not fold this omelette but, instead garnish with a spring onion and serve the omelette cut in half. Serve at once.

Serves 2.

– ITALIAN COUNTRY FRITTATA –

1 courgette (zucchini), diced
1 stick celery, diced
60 ml (2 fl oz / ¼ cup) vegetable oil
2 tomatoes, skinned, seeded and chopped
salt and pepper
4 eggs
2 tablespoons grated Parmesan cheese
1 teaspoon chopped fresh basil
extra Parmesan cheese for sprinkling
fresh mint sprigs, to garnish

Put courgette (zucchini) and celery into a large frying pan with half the oil and cook gently over low heat for 5 minutes. Add tomatoes and salt and pepper and simmer for a further 15 minutes, stirring occasionally.

In a bowl, beat eggs with cheese and basil. Add remaining oil to pan and heat for 1 minute, then pour in egg mixture and cook for 4 minutes over low heat. Carefully turn mixture and continue cooking other side for 4 minutes. Cut into quarters and sprinkle with Parmesan cheese. Garnish with fresh mint sprigs and serve at once.

Serves 4.

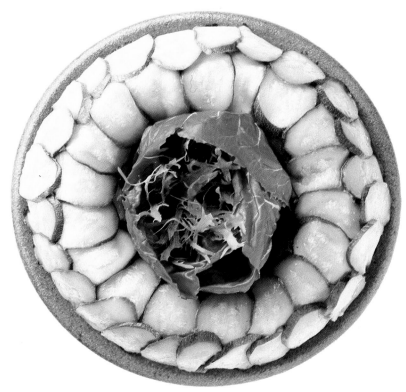

—— MEDITERRANEAN SAUCE ——

1 aubergine (eggplant)
salt
4 tablespoons olive oil
1 onion, chopped
1 clove garlic, crushed
1 small green pepper (capsicum), seeded
1 small red pepper (capsicum), seeded
1 small yellow pepper (capsicum), seeded
4 tomatoes, peeled and roughly chopped
salt and pepper
½ teaspoon dried oregano

Cut aubergine (eggplant) into strips, put into a colander and sprinkle with salt. Leave for 1 hour.

Pat aubergine slices dry with absorbent kitchen paper.

In a large frying pan, heat oil. Add onion and garlic. Cook gently until soft. Add aubergine (eggplant) strips. Cook for 5 minutes, stirring.

Cut peppers (capsicums) into strips, add to pan and cook for 5 minutes. Stir in tomatoes, salt, pepper and oregano. Cover pan and cook gently for 20 minutes. Serve with spaghetti.

Serves 4.

—— COURGETTE PASTA MOULD ——

3 medium courgettes (zucchini), thinly sliced
125 g (4 oz/2¼ cups) wholewheat pasta wheat ears
6 teaspoons vegetable oil
1 large onion, finely chopped
4 tomatoes, peeled and chopped
3 teaspoons tomato purée (paste)
2 teaspoons chopped fresh oregano
1 egg, beaten
salt and pepper
30 g (1 oz/6 teaspoons) butter
radicchio and endive leaves, to serve

In a saucepan of boiling water, cook courgettes (zucchini) for 3-4 minutes until just tender. Drain, then rinse with cold water. Spread out on a tea towel.

In a large pan of boiling salted water, cook wheat ears until just tender. Drain. Meanwhile, heat oil in a frying pan. Add onion and cook gently until soft. In a bowl, mix together pasta, onion, tomatoes, tomato purée (paste), oregano and egg. Season to taste with salt and pepper.

Preheat oven to 200C (400F/Gas 6). Thoroughly butter a ring mould, then line with courgette (zucchini) slices, overlapping them like tiles on a roof.

Fill mould with pasta mixture. Cover with overlapping courgette (zucchini) slices. Dot top with butter. Cover with foil. Bake in the oven for 40 minutes. Turn out onto a serving plate. Serve hot or cold with radicchio and endive leaves.

Serves 6.

BROCCOLI PASTA SOUFFLÉ

250 g (8 oz) broccoli	
125 g (4 oz/2 cups) pasta shells	
45 g (1½ oz/9 teaspoons) butter	
45 g (1½ oz/⅓ cup) plain flour	
315 ml (10 fl oz/1¼ cups) milk	
90 g (3 oz/¾ cup) grated Cheddar cheese	
salt and pepper	
freshly grated nutmeg	
3 eggs, separated, plus 1 extra egg white	

Divide broccoli into small flowerets. Cook in boiling salted water until just tender but still crisp. Drain.

In a large saucepan of boiling salted water, cook pasta shells until tender.

Preheat oven to 200C (400F/Gas 6). Grease a 1 litre (32 fl oz/4 cup) soufflé dish. In a saucepan, melt butter and stir in flour. Cook for 2 minutes, stirring over gentle heat. Gradually add milk and cook, stirring, until sauce thickens. Simmer gently for 5 minutes, then stir in grated cheese. Season with salt, pepper and nutmeg. Leave for a few minutes to cool slightly.

In a large bowl, whisk egg whites until stiff but not dry. Stir egg yolks into cheese sauce, then add broccoli and pasta. Stir 1 tablespoon of egg white into mixture, then gently fold in the rest. Pour mixture into soufflé dish. Bake in the oven for about 30 minutes until the soufflé is well risen, golden brown and just set in the middle. Serve at once.

Serves 4.

Note: This mixture may be cooked in individual soufflé dishes and baked for 20 minutes.

VEGETARIAN BOLOGNESE

185 g (6 oz/1 cup) brown lentils	
125 g (4 oz/⅔ cup) split peas	
2 tablespoons vegetable oil	
1 onion, finely chopped	
1 clove garlic, crushed	
1 carrot, finely chopped	
1 stick celery, finely chopped	
440 g (14 oz) can tomatoes	
1 teaspoon dried oregano	
salt and pepper	
Parmesan cheese, to serve	
sprig of parsley, to garnish	

In a saucepan, bring 625 ml (20 fl oz/2½ cups) water to the boil. Stir in lentils and split peas. Simmer, covered, for about 40 minutes, or until all liquid has been absorbed and lentils and peas are soft.

In a saucepan, heat oil. Add onion, garlic, carrot and celery. Cook over a low heat, stirring occasionally, until soft. Stir in chopped tomatoes and oregano. Season with salt and pepper. Cover pan and simmer gently for 5 minutes.

Add lentils and split peas to pan. Cook, stirring, until well combined and heated through. Serve with wholewheat spaghetti sprinkled with Parmesan cheese and garnished with parsley.

Serves 4-6.

MARINATED STUFFED LEAVES

8 small spinach leaves
8 small Chinese leaves
8 small radicchio leaves
1 yellow pepper (capsicum)
marjoram and parsley sprigs, to garnish
MARINADE:
1 teaspoon finely grated orange peel
3 teaspoons freshly squeezed orange juice
90 ml (3 fl oz / ⅓ cup) olive oil
3 teaspoons chopped fresh marjoram
½ teaspoon each salt and black pepper
1 teaspoon Dijon mustard
1 teaspoon caster sugar
FILLING:
250 g (8 oz / 1 cup) full fat soft cheese
1 clove garlic, crushed
6 teaspoons chopped fresh parsley

Plunge spinach leaves into boiling water for 30 seconds; refresh in cold water. Drain well. Repeat with Chinese and radicchio leaves.

To make marinade, mix all the ingredients together. Pour one-third into a bowl and add radicchio leaves, turning to coat. Place spinach and Chinese leaves in remaining marinade. Cover and leave in a cool place for 2 hours.

To make filling, beat cheese, garlic and parsley together.

Preheat grill, and grill pepper (capsicum) until skin is charred and flesh is tender. Peel and remove stalk and seeds, then purée in a food processor or blender.

Drain leaves, reserving marinade. Take 1 leaf at a time and spread out flat on a board. Place 1 teaspoonful of cheese in centre, fold in edges and roll up firmly. Repeat until all the leaves are used. Place in a serving dish.

Mix pepper (capsicum) and remaining marinade together and pour around leaves in dish. Garnish.

Serves 4.

MIXED VEGETABLE KEBABS

375 g (12 oz) aubergine (eggplant), cut into bite-size pieces
125 g (4 oz) red pepper (capsicum), seeded and cut into 2 cm (¾ in) cubes
125 g (4 oz) yellow pepper (capsicum), seeded and cut into 2 cm (¾ in) cubes
4 small courgettes (zucchini), trimmed and cut into 1 cm (½ in) slices
8 shallots, quartered
16 button mushrooms
16 cherry tomatoes
oregano and parsley sprigs, to garnish
MARINADE:
90 ml (3 fl oz/⅓ cup) olive oil
3 teaspoons raspberry vinegar
½ teaspoon each salt and black pepper
1 teaspoon dry mustard
3 teaspoons light soft brown sugar
3 teaspoons chopped fresh oregano
3 teaspoons chopped fresh parsley

To make marinade, mix oil, vinegar, salt, pepper, mustard, sugar, chopped oregano and parsley together, stirring until well blended.

Put aubergine (eggplant) in a colander or sieve over a bowl, sprinkle with salt, cover with a plate, weight the top and leave for 30 minutes. Rinse thoroughly to remove salt, then press out water.

Add all vegetables to marinade and turn vegetables carefully to coat completely. Cover with plastic wrap and leave to marinate in a cool place for 1 hour.

Meanwhile, soak 8 wooden barbecue skewers. Prepare barbecue or preheat grill.

Thread a mixture of vegetables on to the skewers. Cook 3-5 minutes, brushing with marinade until just tender.

Arrange on a serving dish, garnished with fresh oregano and parsley sprigs.

Serves 4.

RATATOUILLE

1 aubergine (eggplant), thinly sliced

salt

90 ml (3 fl oz/1/3 cup) olive oil

1 red pepper (capsicum), seeded and thinly sliced

1 yellow pepper (capsicum), seeded and thinly sliced

2 onions, thinly sliced

3 courgettes (zucchini), thinly sliced

3 tomatoes, skinned, seeded and thinly sliced

coriander, basil or parsley, to garnish

MARINADE:

6 teaspoons dry red wine

1 clove garlic, crushed

6 teaspoons chopped fresh coriander

6 teaspoons chopped fresh basil

6 teaspoons chopped fresh parsley

1 teaspoon Dijon mustard

1/2 teaspoon salt

1/2 teaspoon black pepper

Arrange aubergine (eggplant) in a colander or sieve over a bowl.

Sprinkle salt between layers, cover with a plate, weight down and leave 30 minutes. Rinse under cold running water and dry the slices on kitchen paper.

Heat oil in a large frying pan, add aubergine (eggplant), peppers (capsicums), onions and courgettes (zucchini) and fry gently 4-5 minutes, stirring occasionally, until almost tender. Add tomatoes and cook for 3-4 minutes, until all the vegetables are tender.

To make marinade, mix wine, garlic, coriander, basil, parsley, mustard, salt and pepper together. Add vegetables and turn in marinade until well coated. Set aside until cold.

Pour into a serving dish and garnish with fresh coriander, parsley or basil leaves.

Serves 6.

SPICED OKRA

375 g (12 oz) okra, stalks removed

4 tomatoes, skinned, seeded and chopped

90 g (3 oz/1/3 cup) strained Greek yogurt

coriander sprigs, to garnish

MARINADE:

1 red chilli, seeded and chopped

1 onion, finely chopped

1 clove garlic, crushed

1 teaspoon ground cumin

1 teaspoon ground coriander

1/2 teaspoon salt

1/2 teaspoon black pepper

1 teaspoon sugar

6 teaspoons olive oil

To make marinade, mix chilli, onion, garlic, cumin, coriander, salt, pepper, sugar and oil together, stirring until thoroughly blended.

Add okra to marinade and turn gently until evenly coated. Cover with plastic wrap and leave in a cool place for 1 hour.

Put tomatoes and 155 ml (5 fl oz/ 2/3 cup) water in a saucepan and bring to the boil. Add okra and marinade and return to the boil, stirring carefully. Cover and cook for 15-20 minutes, until okra is tender.

Pour mixture into a shallow serving dish, add yogurt and stir gently to swirl yogurt. Serve hot or cold, garnished with coriander sprigs.

Serves 4.

TRADITIONAL PIZZA DOUGH

345 g (11 oz/2¾ cups) strong white flour
1 heaped teaspoon salt
15 g (½ oz/3 teaspoons) fresh (compressed) yeast; or 1 teaspoon dried active yeast and 1 teaspoon sugar; or 1 teaspoon easy blend yeast
185 ml (6 fl oz/¾ cup) hand-hot water
1 tablespoon olive oil

Put flour and salt in a large bowl.

In a small bowl, mix fresh yeast with a little water; put in a warm place until frothy. To use dried active yeast, whisk with sugar and a little water; leave until frothy. Add yeast liquid to flour with remaining water and oil. (To use easy blend yeast, mix into flour and salt before adding water and oil.) Mix to a soft dough; knead on floured surface for 10 minutes. Put in a greased bowl, cover; put in a warm place for 45 minutes or until doubled in size.

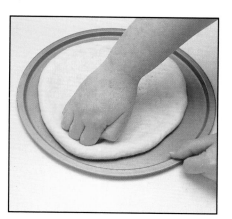

Knock back dough and knead briefly. Oil a 30 cm (12 in) pizza tin. Put dough in centre and press out to edges with knuckles. Pinch up edges to create a rim. Use as recipe instructs.

THREE PEPPER PIZZA

1 quantity Traditional Pizza Dough, shaped and ready for topping
TOPPING:
1 red pepper (capsicum)
1 yellow pepper (capsicum)
1 green pepper (capsicum)
2 tomatoes, skinned
3 tablespoons olive oil
1 onion, finely chopped
1 clove garlic, crushed
salt and pepper
pinch of dried oregano
oregano sprigs and olives, to garnish

Make the topping. Skin peppers (capsicums): spear one at a time with a fork and hold over a gas flame for 5-10 minutes until black and blistered. Alternatively, halve and seed peppers (capsicums). Place under preheated grill until black. Peel skin off with a knife.

Chop red pepper (capsicum); quarter, seed and chop tomatoes. Put in a saucepan with 2 tablespoons oil, onion and garlic. Cook until soft. Preheat oven to 220C (425F/Gas 7). Brush dough with a little oil.

Spread pepper (capsicum) mixture over dough. Season to taste with salt and pepper. Sprinkle with oregano. Cut remaining peppers (capsicums) in strips. Arrange over pizza. Season to taste with salt and pepper. Sprinkle with remaining oil. Bake in the oven for 20 minutes until dough is crisp and golden. Garnish with oregano and olives.

Serves 4.

FOUR CHEESE PIZZA

1 quantity Traditional Pizza Dough, shaped and ready for topping, see page 45
TOPPING:
2 tablespoons olive oil
60 g (2 oz) Mozzarella cheese
60 g (2 oz) Gorgonzola cheese
60 g (2 oz) Fontina or Gruyère cheese
60 g (2 oz / ½ cup) freshly grated Parmesan cheese
salt and pepper
chopped spring onion and extra grated cheese, to garnish

Preheat oven to 220C (425F/Gas 7). Brush dough with 1 tablespoon oil. Cut the 3 cheeses into small cubes. Sprinkle over the dough. Sprinkle over Parmesan, season to taste with salt and pepper. Sprinkle over remaining oil.

Bake in the oven for 20 minutes until cheese is melted and dough is crisp and golden. Garnish with spring onion and extra cheese.

Serves 4.

AUBERGINE & TOMATO PIZZA

1 quantity Traditional Pizza Dough, shaped and ready for topping, see page 45
AUBERGINE TOPPING:
500 g (1 lb) aubergines (eggplants)
1 clove garlic, crushed
3 tablespoons lemon juice
3 tablespoons chopped fresh parsley
2 spring onions, chopped
salt and pepper
TO FINISH:
500 g (1 lb) tomatoes, sliced
1 tablespoon olive oil
2 tablespoons chopped fresh parsley
2 tablespoons freshly grated Parmesan cheese
parsley sprigs, to garnish

First make Aubergine Topping. Preheat oven to 180C (350F/Gas 4). Put aubergines (eggplants) on a baking sheet and bake in the oven for 30 minutes until soft. Cool.

Halve and scoop out soft centres into a bowl. Add garlic, lemon juice, parsley and spring onions. Season to taste with salt and pepper.

Increase oven temperature to 220C (425F/Gas 7). Spread aubergine (eggplant) purée over dough. Arrange sliced tomatoes on top, brush with oil and season to taste with salt and pepper. Sprinkle with chopped parsley and Parmesan cheese. Bake in the oven for 20 minutes. Serve garnished with parsley.

Serves 4.

Note: The aubergine purée may be made in advance and refrigerated for 3-4 days. It is also delicious served as a dip with hot toast or pitta bread.

ARTICHOKE & EMMENTAL PIZZA

1 quantity Traditional Pizza Dough, shaped and ready for topping, see page 45

TOPPING:

3 tablespoons olive oil

440 g (14 oz) can artichoke hearts

salt and pepper

250 g (8 oz / 2 cups) grated Emmental cheese

marjoram leaves and sliced pimento, to garnish

Preheat oven to 220C (425F/Gas 7). Brush the pizza dough with 1 tablespoon of the olive oil.

Drain artichokes and slice thinly. Arrange artichoke slices over dough. Sprinkle with remaining oil; season to taste with salt and pepper. Sprinkle the grated Emmental cheese over the top.

Bake in the oven for 20 minutes until dough is crisp and golden and cheese has melted. Serve at once, garnished with marjoram leaves and sliced pimento.

Serves 4.

LEEK & ONION CALZONI

1 quantity Traditional Pizza Dough, made up to end of step 2, see page 45

1 tablespoon olive oil

beaten egg, to glaze

leek, onion and olive slices, to garnish

FILLING:

3 tablespoons olive oil

2 small leeks, sliced

2 onions, sliced

1 large Spanish onion, sliced

125 ml (4 fl oz / ½ cup) dry white wine

125 ml (4 fl oz / ½ cup) single (light) cream

salt and pepper

freshly grated nutmeg, to taste

125 g (4 oz) stuffed olives, chopped

Make filling. Heat oil and cook leeks and onions gently for 10 minutes until soft. Increase heat, add wine and cook until almost dry.

Reduce heat, add cream and season to taste with salt, pepper and nutmeg. Cook for 2-3 minutes until creamy. Remove from heat, stir in olives and set aside.

Preheat oven to 220C (425F/Gas 7). Grease 2 baking sheets. Divide dough into 2 equal pieces. Roll out both pieces on a lightly floured surface to circles measuring 25 cm (10 in) in diameter. Brush lightly with oil.

Divide filling between the 2 pieces of dough, confining it to one half of each circle. Dampen edges with water, then fold over dough to enclose filling and seal well by pressing with a fork. Transfer to baking sheets, brush with beaten egg and make 2 or 3 air holes with a sharp knife. Bake in the oven for 20 minutes until golden. Serve garnished with leek, onion and olive slices.

Serves 4-6.

STILTON & WALNUT SALAD

2 heads chicory
2 heads Little Gem lettuce, shredded
1 large ripe pear
60 g (2 oz) blue Stilton, grated
walnut halves, to garnish
WALNUT DRESSING:
60 g (2 oz/⅓ cup) walnut pieces
4 tablespoons sunflower oil
2 tablespoons lemon juice
2 tablespoons apple juice
salt and pepper

Chop chicory and put into a bowl with the shredded lettuce. Peel and quarter pear, remove core, then cut into small slices. Add to bowl with cheese.

To make the dressing, put ingredients into a blender and work until smooth. Pour over salad and toss together. Divide between 4 plates, and serve garnished with walnuts.

Serves 4.

MALAYSIAN SALAD

250 g (8 oz) white cabbage, shredded
125 g (4 oz) thin green beans, cut into
2.5 cm (1 in) lengths
½ small cauliflower, divided into flowerets
125 g (4 oz) beansprouts, trimmed
½ cucumber
coriander leaves, to garnish
PEANUT SAUCE:
30 g (1 oz) desiccated coconut
155 ml (5 fl oz/⅔ cup) boiling water
3 tablespoons peanut butter
2 teaspoons soy sauce
juice of ½ lime
¼ teaspoon chilli powder

To make sauce, place coconut in a bowl, pour over boiling water and leave to soak for 15 minutes.

Bring a large saucepan of water to the boil, add cabbage, beans and cauliflower and simmer for 2-3 minutes. Drain vegetables thoroughly, arrange on a platter or 4 individual plates. Scatter over beansprouts. Cut strips of skin from cucumber with a canelle knife, then slice the cucumber and arrange over salad.

Strain coconut milk into a bowl, discard the coconut, and add remaining sauce ingredients; mix well. Spoon onto centre of salad or serve separately. Garnish the salad with coriander leaves.

Serves 4.

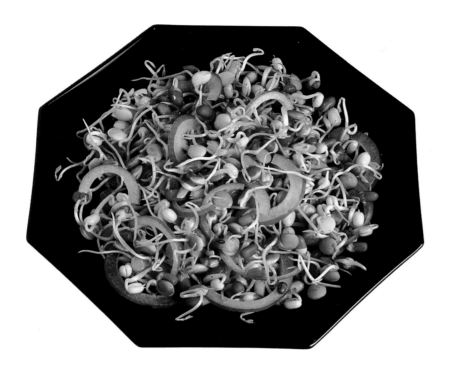

SPROUTED BEAN SALAD

60 g (2 oz) aduki beans	
60 g (2 oz / ⅓ cup) mung beans	
60 g (2 oz / ⅓ cup) green lentils	
1 purple onion	
HONEY MUSTARD DRESSING:	
60 ml (2 fl oz / ¼ cup) mayonnaise	
2 tablespoons sunflower oil	
1 tablespoon clear honey	
1 tablespoon prepared mild mustard	
1 tablespoon lemon juice	
salt and pepper	

Start this salad 4-6 days before you want to serve it. Put each of the beans in a bowl, cover with water and leave to soak overnight. Drain and put each variety into a wide-neck jar. Cover with muslin, secure with elastic bands and place all the jars in a warm, dark place such as an airing cupboard.

Twice a day, fill the jars with water, drain through the muslin to rinse the beans. The beans will have sprouted in 4-6 days. Remove the sprouted beans from the jars and rinse again.

To make the dressing, beat all the ingredients together in a bowl until the honey is evenly blended. Slice the onion and mix with the sprouted beans. Place in a serving dish and add the dressing. Toss the salad until all the sprouts are coated and serve immediately.

Serves 6 as a side salad.

Note: The sprouted beans can be stored in the refrigerator for up to 4 days.

JADE SALAD

250 g (8 oz / 1⅓ cups) long grain rice	
250 g (8 oz) frozen chopped spinach, thawed	
1 bunch spring onions, trimmed	
2 tablespoons chopped fresh parsley	
salt and pepper	
60 ml (2 fl oz / ¼ cup) vinaigrette dressing	

Cook the rice in a saucepan of boiling salted water for 10-12 minutes until tender. Drain, rinse with fresh boiling water, then drain.

Squeeze as much water from spinach as possible, then put into a salad bowl. Reserve 2 spring onions to cut into tassels, then finely chop the rest. Add to the bowl with the spinach, parsley and seasoning. Add rice and, while still warm, stir in dressing and mix. Allow salad to cool completely, then chill before serving. Serve garnished with spring onion tassels.

Serves 6.

TABBOULEH

185 g (6 oz) bulgar wheat
60 ml (2 fl oz/¼ cup) lemon juice
60 ml (2 fl oz/¼ cup) virgin olive oil
1 tablespoon finely chopped Spanish onion
6 spring onions, finely chopped
90 g (3 oz) bunch flat leaf parsley, chopped
30 g (1 oz) fresh mint, chopped
salt and pepper
1 cos lettuce
cherry tomatoes and parsley sprigs, to garnish

Put bulgar into a bowl, cover with warm water and leave to soak for 30 minutes. Squeeze out excess water and put bulgar into a bowl. Add lemon juice, oil, onion, spring onions, parsley and mint and season to taste with salt and pepper. Mix together, then chill for a least 1 hour.

To serve, arrange cos lettuce leaves around the edge of a platter, spoon salad in the centre and garnish with cherry tomatoes and sprigs of parsley.

Serves 6.

WALDORF SALAD

3 red eating apples
3 tablespoons lemon juice
5 sticks celery
60 g (2 oz/⅓ cup) walnuts, roughly chopped
½ teaspoon caraway seeds
125 ml (4 fl oz/½ cup) mayonnaise
walnut halves and celery leaves, to garnish

Cut apples into quarters and remove cores; dice them and put into a bowl with lemon juice.

Thinly slice celery, add to the apple with the walnuts and caraway seeds. Mix together, then stir in the mayonnaise.

Spoon the apple and celery into a bowl and serve garnished with walnut halves and celery leaves.

Serves 6 as a side salad.

— BEETROOT & ONION SALAD —

500 g (1 lb) cooked beetroot
2 shallots, finely chopped
60 ml (2 fl oz / ½ cup) vinaigrette dressing
1 lettuce, separated into leaves
½ small onion, cut into thin rings
chopped fresh parsley, to garnish

Cut beetroot into matchsticks. Put into a bowl and mix with shallots and dressing. Leave to marinate for 2 hours.

Line a serving bowl with lettuce leaves, spoon beetroot on top and scatter over onion rings. Serve garnished with chopped parsley.

Serves 4-6.

— WHOLEWHEAT PASTA SALAD —

125 g (4 oz) wholewheat pasta shapes
185 g (6 oz) shelled broad beans
250 g (8 oz) broccoli flowerets
90 g (3 oz) mange tout (snow peas), trimmed
3 tomatoes, diced
60 ml (2 fl oz / ¼ cup) garlic vinaigrette
herb sprigs, to garnish

Cook pasta in a saucepan of boiling salted water for 12-15 minutes until just tender. Drain, rinse with cold water, and drain again. Put into a bowl.

Cook broad beans in a saucepan of boiling salted water for 15 minutes until tender; drain. Cool slightly, then remove skins while still warm.

Steam broccoli and mange tout (snow peas) in a colander over a saucepan of boiling water for 3 minutes. Leave vegetables to cool, then add to the pasta with the tomatoes. Spoon over the vinaigrette and toss well. Transfer salad to a serving dish and serve garnished with sprigs of herbs.

Serves 4-6.

WINTER RED SALAD

1 oakleaf lettuce or other red lettuce
1 head radicchio
1 purple onion, sliced
125 g (4 oz) red cabbage, shredded
185 g (6 oz) cooked beetroot, diced
pomegranate seeds, to garnish
WALNUT VINAIGRETTE:
2 tablespoons walnut oil
1 tablespoon virgin olive oil
1 tablespoon red wine vinegar
½ teaspoon Dijon mustard
pinch sugar
salt and pepper

Arrange salad leaves in a bowl. Add the onion, cabbage and beetroot.

To make the dressing, mix all the ingredients together in a bowl or screw-top jar, add to salad and toss gently. Serve garnished with pomegranate seeds.

Serves 4-6.

WINTER GREEN SALAD

1½ lettuces or mixed salad leaves
250 g (8 oz) broccoli flowerets, trimmed
1 bunch watercress, trimmed
440 g (14 oz) can artichoke hearts, drained
1 bulb fennel, finely sliced
1 green pepper (capsicum), seeded and sliced
GREEN GODDESS DRESSING:
155 ml (5 fl oz / ⅔ cup) mayonnaise
2 spring onions, finely chopped
2 tablespoons chopped fresh parsley
1 tablespoon tarragon vinegar
1 tablespoon lemon juice
1 clove garlic, crushed
3 tablespoons thick sour cream
salt and pepper

Tear the lettuces into small pieces and put into a serving bowl. Blanch broccoli in a saucepan of boiling water for 2 minutes. Drain, cool, then add to the lettuce with the watercress. Halve the artichoke hearts and add to the salad bowl with the sliced fennel and pepper (capsicum). Toss gently together.

To make the dressing, mix all the ingredients together in a bowl. Spoon a little dressing over the salad, and serve the remainder separately.

Serves 6-8.

Variation: Substitute cauliflower for the broccoli, if preferred.

COCONUT LIME DRESSING

60 g (2 oz) creamed coconut
1 teaspoon grated fresh root ginger
2 teaspoons finely grated lime peel
3 teaspoons freshly squeezed lime juice
1 teaspoon clear honey
125 g (4 oz/½ cup) strained Greek yogurt

Put coconut and 6 teaspoons boiling water in a bowl, stirring until smooth. Leave until cold.

Stir in ginger, lime peel and juice, honey and yogurt until well blended.

Cover with plastic wrap and leave in a cool place until required.

Use to toss mixed fresh fruit for a fruit salad, on an onion and potato salad or a grape, pear and cream cheese salad.

Makes 155 ml (5 fl oz/⅔ cup).

Variations: Replace lime peel and juice with lemon, orange or grapefruit peel and juice.

ORANGE & SESAME DRESSING

1 teaspoon tarragon and thyme mustard
¼ teaspoon salt
½ teaspoon black pepper
1 teaspoon finely grated orange peel
140 ml (4½ fl oz/½ cup) sesame seed oil
6 teaspoons freshly squeezed orange juice
3 teaspoons sesame seeds
3 teaspoons chopped fresh tarragon
2 teaspoons chopped fresh thyme

Put mustard, salt, pepper, orange peel and oil in a bowl and whisk together until well blended.

Add orange juice and sesame seeds and whisk until mixture becomes cloudy and slightly thick. Cover with plastic wrap and leave in a cool place.

Just before using, stir in tarragon and thyme.

Serve with bitter leaf salads such as endive, radicchio, watercress and sorrel.

Makes 155 ml (5 fl oz/⅔ cup).

Variations: Replace the grated orange peel and the juice with either lemon, lime or grapefruit peel and juice.

SAFFRON & PISTACHIO DRESSING — GAZPACHO DRESSING

| 1 teaspoon saffron strands or good pinch powdered saffron |
| 2 teaspoons clear honey |
| ¼ teaspoon salt |
| ½ teaspoon black pepper |
| 75 ml (2½ fl oz/⅓ cup) almond oil |
| 2 teaspoons orange flower water |
| 6 teaspoons white wine vinegar |
| 3 teaspoons finely chopped pistachio nuts |

Mix together saffron and honey with 3 teaspoons boiling water until well blended. Leave until cold.

Add salt, pepper and almond oil and whisk until evenly mixed. Whisk in orange flower water and vinegar until cloudy and slightly thick. Cover with plastic wrap and leave the dressing in a cool place until ready to use.

Just before using, stir in pistachio nuts. Use to mix with pasta, rice, cabbage or leaf salads.

Makes 155 ml (5 fl oz/⅔ cup).

Variations: Replace pistachio nuts with pine nuts.

| 2 tomatoes, skinned, seeded and chopped |
| 90 g (3 oz/1½ cups) soft breadcrumbs |
| 60 ml (2 fl oz/¼ cup) sherry vinegar |
| 90 ml (3 fl oz/⅓ cup) olive oil |
| 3 teaspoons finely chopped shallots |
| 3 teaspoons finely chopped red pepper (capsicum) |
| 3 teaspoons finely chopped green pepper (capsicum) |
| 5 cm (2 in) piece cucumber, peeled and finely chopped |
| 2 teaspoons chilli and garlic sauce |
| ¼ teaspoon salt |
| ½ teaspoon black pepper |
| 1 teaspoon Dijon mustard |

Put chopped tomatoes, breadcrumbs, sherry vinegar and olive oil into a bowl and beat together with a wooden spoon until well blended.

Stir in shallots, peppers (capsicums), cucumber, chilli and garlic sauce, salt, pepper and mustard until well blended. Alternatively, using a food processor fitted with a metal blade, add all the ingredients and process until puréed. Cover with plastic wrap and chill the dressing until required.

Makes 250 ml (8 fl oz/1 cup).

GREEK DRESSING

4 new potatoes, about 125 g (4 oz), cooked
2 cloves garlic, crushed
4 teaspoons ground almonds
140 ml (4½ fl oz / ½ cup) almond oil
juice of 1 orange
6 teaspoons white wine vinegar
6 teaspoons chopped fresh mint

Mash potatoes in a bowl, then add garlic, almonds and oil, beating well with wooden spoon until smooth. Alternatively, use a food processor fitted with a metal blade and process until quite smooth.

Stir in orange juice, vinegar and mint until evenly blended. If dressing is too thick, thin with cold water. Cover with plastic wrap and chill until required.

Serve with fried aubergine (eggplant) slices or with globe artichokes. This dressing can also be served as a dip with a selection of raw vegetables.

Serves 4.

MUSHROOM DIP

60 g (2 oz/¼ cup) unsalted butter
185 g (6 oz) button mushrooms, roughly chopped
¼ teaspoon Tabasco sauce
¼ teaspoon salt
½ teaspoon black pepper
6 teaspoons chopped fresh spring onions
1 teaspoon finely grated lime peel
2 teaspoons freshly squeezed lime juice
90 g (3 oz/⅓ cup) full fat soft cheese
4 teaspoons chopped fresh chervil
chervil sprigs, and lime slices, to garnish

Melt butter in a saucepan, add mushrooms and fry for 1 minute.

Place mushrooms, Tabasco sauce, salt, pepper and spring onions in a food processor fitted with a metal blade and process until puréed. Add lime peel, juice, cheese and chervil and process until well blended and smooth. Cover with plastic wrap and chill until ready to serve.

Serve in a dish garnished and surrounded by Melba toast, biscuits or raw salad ingredients, such as radishes, small cauliflower flowerets, courgette (zucchini) sticks, celery and tomatoes. Also serve as a thick dressing with mixed salads.

Makes 315 ml (10 fl oz/1¼ cups).

ASPARAGUS & AVOCADO SALAD

500 g (1 lb) asparagus spears
1 ripe avocado
4 teaspoons chopped pistachio nuts or walnuts
fennel sprigs and orange segments, to garnish
MARINADE:
125 ml (4 fl oz/½ cup) walnut oil
6 teaspoons freshly squeezed orange juice
2 teaspoons grated orange peel
2 teaspoons light soft brown sugar
½ teaspoon salt
½ teaspoon black pepper
2 teaspoons Dijon mustard
6 teaspoons chopped fresh fennel

Trim asparagus spears and, using a sharp knife, peel outside skin off each stem. Cook asparagus in large shallow saucepan of boiling salted water for 5-8 minutes, until tender. Drain and cool.

To make marinade, mix oil, orange juice, peel, sugar, salt, pepper, mustard and fennel together, stirring until well blended.

Place asparagus spears in a shallow dish, pour over marinade and turn each spear in marinade to coat evenly. Cover with plastic wrap and leave in a cool place for 1 hour or until ready to serve.

Lift out asparagus and arrange on 4 individual serving plates. Peel and dice avocado and add to marinade with pistachios or walnuts, turning gently.

Spoon avocado and nut mixture over centres of asparagus spears and garnish with sprigs of fennel and orange segments.

Serves 4.

HERB CUCUMBER FRAIS

1 cucumber
250 g (8 oz/1 cup) fromage frais
dill sprigs and chive flowers, to garnish
MARINADE:
4 teaspoons chopped fresh tarragon
4 teaspoons chopped fresh dill
4 teaspoons snipped fresh chives
½ teaspoon salt
½ teaspoon black pepper
½ teaspoon dry mustard
6 teaspoons red vermouth

Using a canelle cutter, cut off thin strips of cucumber peel to make a ridge effect. Cut cucumber in half lengthwise, scoop out seeds and cut cucumber into 0.5 cm (¼ in) slices.

Bring 155 ml (5 fl oz/⅔ cup) water to boil in a pan, add cucumber and cook for 1 minute. Drain.

To make marinade, mix tarragon, dill, chives, salt, pepper, mustard and vermouth together. Add cucumber and turn gently in marinade to coat. Cover with plastic wrap and leave in a cool place for 2 hours.

Just before serving, gently stir in fromage frais until evenly mixed. Place cucumber mixture in a serving dish and garnish with sprigs of dill and chive flowers.

Serves 4.

CHOW MEIN SALAD

125 g (4 oz) Chinese medium egg noodles
125 g (4 oz) mange tout (snow peas)
185 g (6 oz) fresh beansprouts
½ a bunch of spring onions, chopped
1 red pepper (capsicum), seeded and sliced
125 g (4 oz) button mushrooms, sliced
1 small Little Gem lettuce, shredded

DRESSING: 4 tablespoons sunflower oil
2 tablespoons lemon juice
3 teaspoons soy sauce
2.5 cm (1 in) piece of fresh root ginger
2 tablespoons sesame seeds

Break up noodles and cook in boiling, salted water for 5-6 minutes.

Drain noodles and leave to cool. Top and tail mange tout (snow peas), then break in half and put into a bowl. Pour over enough boiling water to cover and leave to stand for 2 minutes; drain and cool. Put noodles and mange tout (snow peas) into a salad bowl and add remaining salad ingredients.

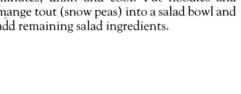

In a bowl, combine oil, lemon juice and soy sauce. Peel and cut ginger into very thin slivers and add to bowl. Mix ingredients well together and pour over salad. Toss well together. Sprinkle with sesame seeds just before serving.

Serves 6-8.

SUMMER VEGETABLE SALAD

375 g (12 oz) aubergine (eggplant), diced
salt and pepper
3 tablespoons olive oil
1 Spanish onion, sliced
375 g (12 oz) courgettes (zucchini), sliced
1 red pepper (capsicum), seeded and cut into chunks
1 green pepper (capsicum), seeded and cut into chunks
1 yellow pepper (capsicum), seeded and cut into chunks
3 tomatoes, skinned and chopped
1 tablespoon chopped fresh basil
1 tablespoon chopped fresh parsley, if desired

Put aubergine (eggplant) into a colander, sprinkle with salt and leave to stand for 30 minutes. Rinse, drain and pat dry.

Heat oil in a large frying pan, add aubergine (eggplant) and onion and cook over medium heat for 5 minutes. Add courgettes (zucchini) and peppers (capsicums); cook over a low heat for 15 minutes, turning occasionally until tender.

Transfer vegetables to a bowl, stir in tomatoes, basil and seasoning. Leave to cool, then chill. Serve sprinkled with chopped parsley, if desired.

Serves 6.

POTATO SALAD

750 g (1½ lb) new potatoes, scrubbed
½ a bunch of spring onions, chopped
1 tablespoon chopped fresh parsley
1 teaspoon chopped fresh marjoram
1 tablespoon chopped fresh dill
sprigs of marjoram, to garnish

YOGURT DRESSING: 5 tablespoons natural yogurt
3 tablespoons mayonnaise
2 teaspoons lemon juice
1 teaspoon Dijon mustard
salt and pepper

Cook potatoes in boiling, salted water until tender; drain and leave to cool.

Slice potatoes thickly and put into a serving bowl. Reserve a little of the chopped spring onions and fresh herbs for garnishing. Add remaining onions and fresh herbs to potatoes in bowl and toss together lightly until combined.

Mix together ingredients for yogurt dressing. Pour over the salad and mix lightly. Serve chilled, garnished with reserved chopped spring onions and chopped fresh mixed herbs and sprigs of marjoram.

Serves 6.

MIXED LEAF SALAD

½ a head each of 2 different types of lettuce
    such as cos, webb's, iceberg, oakleaf
1 avocado
2 teaspoons lemon juice
1 green pepper (capsicum), seeded and sliced
½ a cucumber, sliced
½ a bunch of spring onions, chopped
watercress, trimmed
curly endive
3 sticks celery, chopped

DRESSING: 6 teaspoons walnut oil
6 teaspoons sunflower oil
3 teaspoons white wine vinegar
½ teaspoon Dijon mustard
salt and pepper

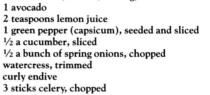

Put lettuce into a large salad bowl. Halve the avocado, remove the stone, then peel. Cut flesh into slices and coat with lemon juice, then add to bowl. Add remaining salad ingredients.

In a bowl, mix together dressing ingredients. Pour over the salad and toss lightly until thoroughly coated with dressing.

Serves 6-8.

CLASSIC SWISS FONDUE

1 clove garlic, halved
250 ml (8 fl oz/1 cup) dry white wine
1 teaspoon lemon juice
250 g (8 oz/2 cups) grated Gruyère cheese
250 g (8 oz/2 cups) grated Emmental cheese
2 teaspoons cornflour
2 tablespoons kirsch
pinch of white pepper
pinch of freshly grated nutmeg
cubes of French bread, to serve

Rub the inside of the fondue pot with cut clove of garlic.

Pour in wine and lemon juice and heat gently until bubbling. Reduce the heat to low and gradually stir in grated cheeses with a wooden spoon, then continue to heat until cheeses melt, stirring frequently.

In a small bowl, blend cornflour smoothly with kirsch, then stir into cheese mixture and continue to cook for 2-3 minutes until mixture is thick and smooth, stirring frequently. Do not allow fondue to boil. Season with pepper and nutmeg. Serve with cubes of French bread.

Serves 4-6.

CURRIED CHEESE FONDUE

1 clove garlic, halved
155 ml (5 fl oz/⅔ cup) dry white wine
1 teaspoon lemon juice
2 teaspoons curry paste
250 g (8 oz/2 cups) grated Gruyère cheese
185 g (6 oz/1½ cups) grated Cheddar cheese
1 teaspoon cornflour
2 tablespoons dry sherry
pieces of Nan bread, to serve

Rub the inside of the fondue pot with cut clove of garlic.

Pour in wine and lemon juice and heat gently until bubbling. Reduce the heat to low, add curry paste and gradually stir in grated cheeses, then continue to heat until cheeses melt, stirring frequently.

In a small bowl, blend cornflour smoothly with sherry, then stir into cheese mixture and continue to cook for 2-3 minutes until mixture is thick and smooth, stirring frequently. Do not allow fondue to boil. Serve with pieces of Nan bread.

Serves 4-6.

SOMERSET FONDUE

½ a small onion
250 ml (8 fl oz/1 cup) dry cider
1 teaspoon lemon juice
375 g (12 oz/3 cups) grated Cheddar cheese
½ teaspoon dry mustard
3 teaspoons cornflour
3 tablespoons apple juice
pinch of white pepper
wedges of apple and cubes of crusty bread, to serve

Rub the inside of the fondue pot with cut side of onion.

Pour in cider and lemon juice and heat gently until bubbling. Reduce the heat to low and gradually stir in grated cheese, then continue to heat until cheese melts, stirring frequently.

In a small bowl, blend mustard and cornflour smoothly with apple juice. Stir into cheese mixture and continue to cook for 2-3 minutes until mixture is thick and creamy, stirring frequently. Season with pepper. Serve with wedges of apple and cubes of crusty bread.

Serves 4-6.

DUTCH FONDUE

½ a small onion
250 ml (8 fl oz/1 cup) milk
500 g (1 lb/4 cups) grated Gouda cheese
2 teaspoons caraway seeds
3 teaspoons cornflour
3 tablespoons gin
pepper
light rye bread and button mushrooms, to serve

Rub the inside of the fondue pot with cut side of onion.

Add milk and heat until bubbling, then gradually stir in cheese. Continue to heat until cheese melts, stirring frequently.

Stir in caraway seeds. In a small bowl, blend cornflour smoothly with gin, then stir into cheese mixture and cook for 2-3 minutes until smooth and creamy, stirring frequently. Season with pepper. Serve with cubes of rye bread and mushrooms.

Serves 4-6.

PLOUGHMAN'S FONDUE

ROSÉ FONDUE

1 clove garlic, halved
315 ml (10 fl oz/1¼ cups) beer
250 g (8 oz/2 cups) grated Red Leicester cheese
   or orange-coloured Cheddar
250 g (8 oz/2 cups) grated Cheddar cheese
3 teaspoons plain flour
1 teaspoon dry mustard
pepper
cubes of granary or white bread and pickles, to serve

Rub the inside of the fondue pot with cut clove of garlic. Add beer and heat until bubbling.

1 clove garlic, halved
250 ml (8 fl oz/1 cup) rosé wine
125 g (4 oz/1 cup) grated Gruyère cheese
250 g (8 oz/2 cups) grated red-veined Cheddar cheese
3 teaspoons cornflour
2 tablespoons kirsch
cubes of sesame-coated French bread, to serve

Rub the inside of the fondue pot with cut clove of garlic. Add wine and heat until bubbling.

Toss grated cheeses in the flour and mustard until well combined.

Gradually stir in cheeses and continue to heat gently until melted, stirring frequently.

Over a low heat, add cheeses to the beer and continue to heat, stirring all the time until mixture is smooth. Season with pepper. Serve with cubes of granary or white bread and pickles.

Serves 4-6.

In a small bowl, blend cornflour smoothly with kirsch and stir into cheese mixture. Cook for 2-3 minutes until smooth and thickened, stirring frequently. Serve with cubes of French bread.

Serves 4-6.

CRICKETER'S FONDUE

15 g (½ oz/3 teaspoons) butter
1 small onion, finely chopped
250 ml (8 fl oz/1 cup) light ale
500 g (1 lb/4 cups) grated Lancashire cheese
4 teaspoons cornflour
5 tablespoons single (light) cream
cauliflower flowerets, radishes and mushrooms, to
  serve

Heat butter in a saucepan, add onion and cook gently until soft. Pour in ale and heat until bubbling.

Over a low heat, stir in the cheese and continue to heat until cheese has melted, stirring frequently.

In a small bowl, blend cornflour smoothly with cream, add to cheese mixture and cook for 2-3 minutes until smooth and thickened, stirring frequently. Pour into a fondue pot. Serve with cauliflower flowerets, radishes and mushrooms.

Serves 4-6.

FONDUE NORMANDE

1 clove garlic, halved
125 ml (4 fl oz/½ cup) dry white wine
155 ml (5 fl oz/⅔ cup) single (light) cream
375 g (12 oz) Camembert cheese, rind removed
3 teaspoons cornflour
4 tablespoons Calvados brandy
cubes of French bread and chunks of apple, to serve

Rub the inside of fondue pot with cut side of garlic. Pour in wine and cream and heat until bubbling.

Cut cheese into small pieces, then add to the pot and stir over a gentle heat until melted.

In a small bowl, blend cornflour smoothly with Calvados, then add to cheese mixture and continue to cook for 2-3 minutes until thick and creamy, stirring frequently. Serve with cubes of French bread and chunks of apple.

Serves 4-6.

HIGHLAND FONDUE

1 small onion, finely chopped
15 g (½ oz/3 teaspoons) butter
250 ml (8 fl oz/1 cup) milk
500 g (1 lb/4 cups) grated Scottish or mature Cheddar cheese
3 teaspoons cornflour
4 tablespoons whisky
cubes of rye and onion bread, to serve

Put onion and butter into a saucepan and cook over a gentle heat until soft. Add milk and heat until bubbling.

Gradually stir in cheese and continue to cook until melted, stirring frequently.

In a small bowl, blend cornflour smoothly with whisky, then stir into cheese mixture and cook 2-3 minutes until thickened, stirring frequently. Pour into the fondue pot and serve with cubes of rye and onion bread.

Serves 4-6.

WELSH FONDUE

30 g (1 oz/6 teaspoons) butter
250 g (8 oz) leeks, trimmed and finely chopped
6 teaspoons plain flour
250 ml (8 fl oz/1 cup) lager
315 g (10 oz/2½ cups) grated Caerphilly cheese
pepper
cubes of crusty bread, to serve

Put butter into a saucepan and melt over a low heat. Add leeks, cover pan and cook gently for 10 minutes until tender.

Stir in flour and cook for 1 minute, then add lager and heat until thickened, stirring all the time.

Gradually add cheese and continue to cook until melted, stirring frequently. Season with pepper. Pour into a fondue pot and serve with cubes of crusty bread.

Serves 4-6.

CAULIFLOWER FRITTERS

1 cauliflower, cut into flowerets
90 g (3 oz/¾ cup) dried breadcrumbs
45 g (1½ oz/⅓ cup) grated Parmesan cheese
1 tablespoon chopped fresh parsley
salt and pepper
2-3 eggs, beaten

CHEESE SAUCE: 15 g (1½ oz/3 teaspoons) butter
15 g (½ oz/6 teaspoons) plain flour
315 ml (10 fl oz/1¼ cups) milk
½ teaspoon prepared mustard
60 g (2 oz/½ cup) grated Cheddar cheese
pinch of cayenne pepper

Par-boil cauliflower in a saucepan of boiling, salted water for 4-5 minutes; drain well.

In a bowl, mix together breadcrumbs, Parmesan cheese and parsley and season with salt and pepper. Dip cauliflower flowerets in beaten egg, then coat in breadcrumb mixture. Put onto a serving plate and set aside until ready to cook in the hot oil.

To make cheese sauce, melt butter in a small saucepan, stir in flour and cook for 1 minute. Remove from heat and add milk slowly. Bring to the boil, stirring, then simmer for 2 minutes. Stir in mustard, cheese, cayenne and season with salt and pepper. Serve hot.

Serves 4-6.

VEGETABLE KEBABS

4 courgettes (zucchini), cut into slices
16 button mushrooms
1 red pepper (capsicum), seeded and cut into chunks
1 green pepper (capsicum), seeded and cut into chunks

CREAMY ONION SAUCE: 125 g (4 oz/½ cup) low fat soft cheese
155 ml (5 fl oz/⅔ cup) natural yogurt
½ a bunch spring onions, finely chopped

BATTER: 2 large eggs
125 g (4 oz/1 cup) plain flour

Thread the vegetables onto 12-16 bamboo skewers.

To make the creamy onion sauce, mix all the ingredients together and put into a serving bowl.

Just before cooking kebabs, make batter. Put eggs into a bowl with 220 ml (7 fl oz/1 cup) iced water and beat until frothy. Add flour and beat until just blended – do not worry if a few lumps are left. Pour into a bowl or jug and stand it in a bowl of ice. To cook kebabs, each person dips a skewer into the batter, then into hot oil to cook until the batter is golden. The kebabs are then eaten with the onion sauce.

Serves 4.

SPICY CHICK PEA BALLS

125 g (4 oz/¾ cup) bulgar wheat
125 ml (4 fl oz/½ cup) boiling water
225 g (8 oz/1¼ cups) chick peas, soaked overnight
2 tablespoons sunflower oil
2 cloves garlic, crushed
½ teaspoon baking powder
1 teaspoon chilli powder
1 teaspoon ground coriander
1 teaspoon ground cumin
salt and pepper

FRESH TOMATO SAUCE: 4 tomatoes, skinned
½ a green pepper (capsicum), halved and seeded
½ a red pepper (capsicum), halved and seeded
1 fresh green chilli, seeded
1 tablespoon fresh coriander, chopped

Put the bulgar wheat into a bowl, pour over the boiling water and leave the wheat to soak for 1 hour. Drain chick peas and put into a food processor with bulgar wheat and remaining ingredients, except those for fresh tomato sauce. Blend for a few minutes until mixture becomes fairly smooth. With your hands, mould the mixture into a 36 small balls and place on a serving dish. These will be speared with a fondue fork and cooked in the hot oil.

To make the fresh tomato sauce, put all the ingredients into a blender or food processor and process until vegetables are finely chopped. Add seasoning, then put into a serving bowl.

Serves 4-6.

SWISS POTATOES

1 kg (2 lb) small new potatoes, scrubbed
2 eggs, beaten
125 g (4 oz/1 cup) herb stuffing mix

GARLIC SAUCE: 125 g (4 oz/2 cups) fresh white
   breadcrumbs
2 cloves garlic
salt and pepper
250 ml (8 fl oz/1 cup) olive oil
4 teaspoons lemon juice
1 tablespoon white wine vinegar

Boil potatoes (in skins) until just tender; drain and cool. Dip in beaten egg, then roll in stuffing mix and set aside.

To make garlic sauce, dampen breadcrumbs with 1 tablespoon water. Put into a blender or food processor with garlic and ½ teaspoon salt and blend together until well mixed. Add oil a little at a time and continue to process until all the oil has been added.

Work the lemon juice and vinegar into the sauce until it forms a smooth, creamy consistency. Season with pepper. Turn mixture into a bowl and serve with the potatoes which are speared and cooked in the hot oil.

Serves 4-6.

Note: Serve the potatoes also with Cheese Sauce, see page 64.

VEGETABLE SAMOSAS

250 g (8 oz) potatoes, cut in even-sized pieces
125 g (4 oz) frozen peas
2 tablespoons corn oil
1 onion, finely chopped
½ teaspoon cumin seeds
1 cm (½ in) piece fresh root ginger, peeled and grated
½ teaspoon turmeric
½ teaspoon Garam Masala
½ teaspoon salt
2 teaspoons lemon juice
125 g (4 oz/1 cup) plain flour
30 g (1 oz/6 teaspoons) butter
2 tablespoons warm milk
vegetable oil for deep frying
mango chutney, to serve
celery leaves and lime twists, to garnish

Boil potatoes in salted water for 15-20 minutes until tender. Drain well, return to saucepan and shake over a low heat for a few moments to dry off. Mash well. Cook peas in boiling, salted water for 4 minutes. Drain well.

Heat corn oil in a frying pan. Add onion, cumin seeds, ginger, turmeric, garam masala and salt and cook gently for 5 minutes. Add mashed potato and peas, then stir in lemon juice. Mix well together and remove from heat and cool.

Sift flour into a bowl. Rub in butter finely until mixture resembles breadcrumbs. Add milk and mix to form a stiff dough. Divide into 6 equal portions.

Form each piece into a ball, then roll out on a lightly floured work surface to form 15 cm (6 in) rounds. Cut each round in half. Divide filling equally between semi-circles of pastry.

Dampen edges of pastry then fold over and seal to form triangular-shaped pasties which enclose the filling completely. Half-fill a deep fat pan or fryer with oil; heat to 190C (375F) or until a cube of day-old bread browns in 40 seconds. Fry samosas, a few at a time, in hot oil for 3-4 minutes until golden. Drain on absorbent kitchen paper. Serve hot. garnished with celery leaves and lime twists, with mango chutney.

Makes 12.

AUBERGINE TAHINI PÂTÉ

1 large aubergine (eggplant)
1 large clove garlic
3 shallots
½-1 teaspoon Garam Masala
3 tablespoons tahini (creamed sesame)
finely grated peel of 1 lemon
3 tablespoons lemon juice
salt
2 teaspoons olive oil
cayenne pepper for sprinkling
lemon slices and sprig of parsley, to garnish
pitta bread, to serve

Preheat oven to 180C (350F/Gas 4). Prick aubergine (eggplant) with a fork.

Bake aubergine (eggplant) in the oven for 30-40 minutes until softened and skin has turned dark brown. Trim ends and peel. Purée flesh in a blender or food processor with garlic, shallots, garam masala, tahini, lemon peel and juice until smooth and evenly combined.   •

Add salt to taste. Turn mixture into a serving bowl, drizzle with olive oil and sprinkle with cayenne pepper. Garnish with lemon slices and sprig of parsley. Serve with warm fingers of pitta bread.

Serves 4-6.

ONION & MUSHROOM BHAJIS

1 onion
60 g (2 oz) button mushrooms
45 g (1½ oz/⅓ cup) brown rice flour
45 g (1½ oz/⅓ cup) plain flour
½ teaspoon turmeric
½ teaspoon hot chilli powder
¼ teaspoon ground cumin
¼ teaspoon ground coriander
¼ teaspoon salt
155 ml (5 fl oz/⅔ cup) natural yogurt
vegetable oil for deep frying
sprig of parsley, to garnish

Peel, quarter and thinly slice onion.

Coarsely chop mushrooms. Put brown rice flour and plain flour in a bowl. Add turmeric, chilli powder, cumin, coriander and salt. Stir in yogurt, onion and mushrooms. Mix well.

Half-fill a deep fat pan or fryer with oil and heat to 190C (375F) or until a cube of day-old bread browns in 40 seconds. Divide mixture into 10 equal portions. Drop spoonfuls of mixture into hot oil and fry for 3-4 minutes until golden brown and cooked through. Drain on absorbent kitchen paper. Serve warm, garnished with a sprig of parsley.

Makes 10.

GUACAMOLE

2 ripe avocados
3 tablespoons lime juice
1 clove garlic, crushed
2 tomatoes, skinned and finely chopped
3 spring onions, finely chopped
1 fresh green chilli, seeded and finely chopped
1 tablespoon chopped fresh coriander leaves
salt and pepper
corn or tortilla chips, to serve
sprig of coriander, to garnish

Cut avocados in half, remove stones and scoop out flesh into a bowl. Mash together with lime juice.

Add garlic, chopped tomatoes, spring onions, chilli, coriander and season with salt and pepper.

Spoon into a bowl and surround with the corn or tortilla chips. Garnish with a sprig of coriander.

Serves 6.

Note: This dip is best made just before serving.

SPANAKOPITA

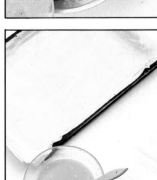

450 g (1 lb) fresh spinach, trimmed
250 g (½ lb) feta cheese
2 tablespoons finely chopped shallots
2 onions, thinly sliced
1 tablespoon finely chopped fresh thyme
1 tablespoon finely chopped rosemary
2 tablespoons finely chopped oregano
2 tablespoons finely chopped fennel
6 eggs
125 ml (4 fl oz / ½ cup) vegetable oil
salt and pepper
14 sheets filo pastry
185 g (6 oz / ¾ cup) butter, melted

Preheat oven to 180C (350F/Gas 4). Steam spinach leaves until limp. Cool, squeeze out all moisture. Combine with cheese, shallots, onion and herbs. In separate bowl, beat together eggs, oil, salt and pepper. Stir into spinach mixture.

Brush a 33 × 23 cm (13 × 9 in) baking tin with a little of the melted butter. Lay a sheet of filo in tin and brush lightly with butter. Repeat using 6 more sheets.

Pour filling over filo layers. Top with remaining filo sheets, brushing with melted butter. Trim and tuck edges to neaten. Bake 45 minutes, or until golden brown. Cut into squares. Serve warm or cold. Store in the refrigerator up to 3 days.

Makes 1 pie.

CREAMY POTATO SKINS

PEARS STUFFED WITH GORGONZOLA

1.5 kg (3 lb) medium potatoes
90 g (3 oz / ⅓ cup) butter, melted
salt
155 ml (5 fl oz / ⅔ cup) thick sour cream
2 tablespoons chopped fresh chives
chopped fresh chives, to garnish

Preheat the oven to 200C (400F/Gas 6). Scrub potatoes and prick with a fork. Bake in the oven for about 1 hour until tender.

8 small ripe pears, peeled
Juice of 2 lemons, in a large bowl
125 g (4 oz) Gorgonzola cheese, softened
60 g (2 oz / ¼ cup) butter, softened
30 g (1 oz / ¼ cup), finely chopped walnuts or pistachio nuts

Slice pears in half, taking care to leave stem intact on one half. Core pears and, with a spoon, remove a tablespoon of the flesh to form a hollow. Immediately immerse pears in bowl with lemon juice to prevent discoloration.

Remove potatoes from the oven and cut each one into quarters. Carefully remove insides leaving about 0.5 cm (¼ in) of flesh on the skins. (The cooked potato can be used in soups). Increase oven temperature to 230C (450F/Gas 8).

In a small bowl, beat together cheese and butter until smooth. Fill each pear half with about a tablespoon of mixture.

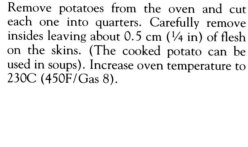

Brush the insides and outsides of potato skins with melted butter. Place on a baking sheet, sprinkle with salt and return to the oven for about 10 minutes or until crisp. Mix thick sour cream with chives and serve with the hot potato skins. Garnish sour cream mixture with chopped chives.

Serves 4-6.

Press pears together and roll in walnuts. Refrigerate at least 2 hours. Serve as first course. Store in the refrigerator up to 3 days.

Makes 8 servings.

BLUE CHEESE DIP & CRACKERS

BLUE CHEESE DIP: 155 g (5 oz/1½ cups) blue cheese, chopped
250 g (8 oz/1 cup) can crushed pineapple, drained
125 ml (4 fl oz/½ cup) sour cream
125 ml (4 fl oz/½ cup) cottage cheese
2 tablespoons fresh chopped chives
Chive sprigs, finely chopped chives, radish slices for decoration

In food processor or blender, blend all ingredients, except chive sprigs.

When just combined, put into bowl or bowls. Cover.

Decorate with chive sprigs, finely chopped chives and radish slices. Store in the refrigerator for up to 1 week.

Makes about 600 g (1¼ lb/2½ cups).

CHEDDAR CHEESE CRACKERS: 125 g (4 oz/⅔ cup) wholemeal flour
2 tablespoons self-raising flour
½ teaspoon salt
¼ teaspoon cayenne pepper
125 g (4 oz/½ cup) cup butter
60 g (2 oz/½ cup) grated Cheddar cheese
1 tablespoon lemon juice
1 egg

Preheat oven 160C (325F/Gas 3). In food processor or blender, combine all ingredients. Blend until dough is formed. Shape mixture into a roll 38 cm (15 in) long. Wrap in cling film. Refrigerate at least 3 hours. Cut roll into slices ½ cm (¼ in) thick, place on lightly greased baking sheets. Bake 15 minutes, or until light golden brown. Cool on baking sheets.

Makes about 60.

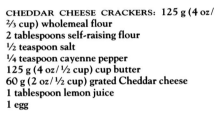

BRAN CRACKERS: 60 g (2 oz/½ cup) unprocessed bran (available in hot cereal or flour section of supermarket)
125 g (4 oz/1 cup) wholewheat flour
1 tablespoon packed brown sugar
125 g (4 oz/½ cup) butter
2 eggs
Pinch salt

Pre-heat oven to 160C (325F/Gas 3). In a food processor or blender, blend bran, flour, sugar and butter. Add eggs and salt. Blend until dough forms. Knead lightly on floured board; press into two 28 × 18 cm (11 × 7 in) tins. Prick surface with a fork. Bake 15 minutes or until light brown. Cut into squares; cool on a wire rack.

Makes about 35.

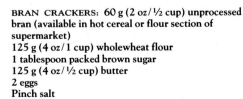

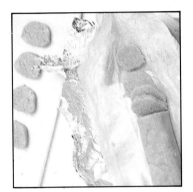

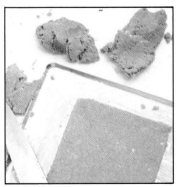

POLANAISE CRUMBLE

250 g (8 oz) cauliflower flowerets
250 g (8 oz) broccoli flowerets

TOPPING: 30 g (1 oz/6 teaspoons) butter
60 g (2 oz/1 cup) soft white breadcrumbs
3 teaspoons chopped fresh parsley
1 hard-boiled egg, sieved

SAUCE: 30 g (1 oz/6 teaspoons) butter
30 g (1 oz/¼ cup) plain flour
315 ml (10 fl oz/1¼ cups) milk
salt and ground black pepper

To make topping, heat butter in a pan, add breadcrumbs and fry until golden. Put in a bowl; add parsley and egg.

To make sauce, put butter, flour, milk and salt and pepper to taste in a saucepan. Whisk together over a moderate heat until thick. Cook for 1-2 minutes, then keep warm.

Cook cauliflower and broccoli in boiling, salted water for 3-4 minutes until just tender. Drain and place in a warmed serving dish. Pour over sauce and sprinkle over topping. Serve hot.

Serves 4-6.

ALMOND BRUSSELS SPROUTS

500 g (1 lb) small Brussels sprouts
30 g (1 oz/6 teaspoons) butter
30 g (1 oz/¼ cup) flaked almonds
1 clove garlic, crushed
1 teaspoon finely grated lemon peel
1 teaspoon lemon juice
½ teaspoon salt
½ teaspoon ground black pepper
lemon twists and herb sprigs, to garnish

Trim stalks off sprouts and make a cut across each one. Cook in boiling, salted water for 4-5 minutes until just tender. Drain well and place in a warmed serving dish.

Meanwhile, melt butter in a small frying pan, add flaked almonds and garlic and fry until almonds are golden brown. Stir in lemon peel and juice and salt and pepper. Mix well.

Sprinkle almond mixture over sprouts and stir gently to mix. Serve immediately, garnished with lemon twists and herb sprigs.

Serves 4.

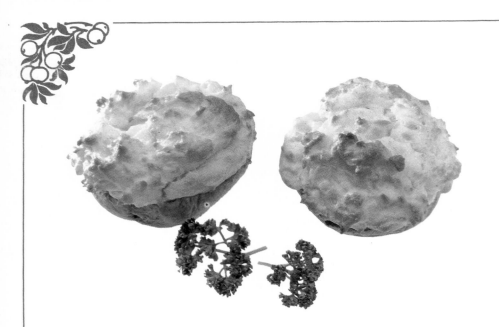

SOUFFLÉ POTATOES

4 large potatoes
30 g (1 oz/6 teaspoons) butter
6 teaspoons single (light) cream
1 teaspoon salt
½ teaspoon ground black pepper
½ teaspoon grated nutmeg
2 eggs, separated

Preheat oven to 220C (425F/Gas 7). Scrub potato skins and remove any 'eyes'. Pierce each potato several times using a small, sharp knife, and arrange on a baking sheet. Cook in the oven for 1 hour, or until potatoes are tender.

Cut each potato in half, carefully scoop out the potato flesh and place in a bowl or an electric mixer fitted with a beater. Replace potato skins on a baking sheet and cook in the oven for 10-15 minutes until crisp and golden. Meanwhile mash or beat potato until smooth, add butter, cream, salt, pepper, nutmeg and egg yolks. Mash or beat until thoroughly blended.

Stiffly whisk egg whites, add to potato and fold in gently, using a spatula, until evenly mixed. Fill each potato skin with mixture and return to oven for 10-15 minutes or until risen and lightly browned. Serve immediately.

Serves 8.

CREAMED SPINACH & CELERY

1 kg (2 lb) spinach
6 sticks celery
30 g (1 oz/6 teaspoons) butter
1 teaspoon grated nutmeg
90 ml (3 fl oz/⅓ cup) double (thick) cream
¼ teaspoon salt
½ teaspoon ground black pepper

Stem and wash spinach; wash and thinly slice celery. Cook celery and spinach separately in boiling, salted water until just tender. Drain each vegetable thoroughly, pressing out excess water from spinach.

Line bases and sides of 8 warmed individual soufflé dishes with a few whole spinach leaves. Chop remaining spinach roughly. Melt butter in a saucepan, add nutmeg, cream and salt and pepper and bring to the boil. Add spinach and toss well.

Half-fill each soufflé dish with spinach mixture, cover each with a layer of celery, reserving a little for garnish, and fill each up to the top with remaining spinach. Press firmly. Just before serving, invert spinach moulds onto a serving plate and garnish with reserved celery slices. Serve warm.

Serves 8.

BAKED POTATO LAYER

1 kg (2 lb) medium potatoes
30 g (1 oz/6 teaspoons) butter
1 clove garlic, crushed
1 teaspoon salt
1 teaspoon ground black pepper
125 g (4 oz/1 cup) grated Cheddar cheese
315 ml (10 fl oz/1¼ cups) milk
155 ml (5 fl oz/⅔ cup) single (light) cream
1 large egg, beaten
parsley sprigs, to garnish

Preheat oven to 190C (375F/Gas 5). Peel and very thinly slice potatoes. Using ½ the butter, lightly grease a 22.5 cm (9 in) shallow ovenproof dish.

Arrange a layer of potato slices over base and up sides of the dish. Sprinkle with some of the garlic, salt, pepper and cheese. Continue to layer until all these ingredients have been used, finishing with a layer of potatoes and a sprinkling of cheese.

Place milk, cream and egg in a bowl and whisk until smooth. Pour over potato layer and dot with remaining butter. Cook in the oven for 1 hour until golden brown and potatoes are tender. Garnish with parsley sprigs and serve hot.

Serves 4-6.

GLAZED CARROTS & ONIONS

12 small, even-sized carrots
16 pickling onions
1 teaspoon salt
60 ml (2 fl oz/¼ cup) vegetable stock
3 teaspoons caster sugar
30 g (1 oz/6 teaspoons) butter
3 teaspoons chopped fresh parsley
herb sprigs, to garnish

Peel and trim carrots to make them even in size, if necessary. Peel and trim onions. Cook carrots and onions separately in boiling, salted water for 5-8 minutes until just tender. Drain well.

Place stock, sugar and butter in a saucepan and heat gently, stirring until sugar has dissolved and butter has melted. Boil rapidly until mixture is reduced by half.

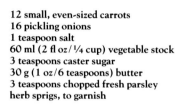

Add carrots, onions and parsley and toss well until thoroughly coated in glaze. Arrange on a warmed serving dish and serve immediately, garnished with sprigs of herbs.

Serves 4.

SPICY SESAME NOODLES

6 teaspoons sesame seeds
3 teaspoons sesame oil
4 teaspoons peanut butter
2 tablespoons soy sauce
2 teaspoons chilli sauce
½ teaspoon sugar
250 g (8 oz) rice vermicelli
carrot flowers and toasted sesame seeds, to garnish

In a dry frying pan, cook sesame seeds over a medium heat until golden brown. Crush slightly.

In a bowl, or food processor, mix together sesame seeds, sesame oil, peanut butter, soy sauce, chilli sauce, sugar and 60 ml (2 fl oz/¼ cup) water. Set aside.

Put rice vermicelli into a bowl. Pour over enough boiling water to cover. Leave to soak for 10 minutes, then drain thoroughly. Put drained vermicelli and sesame sauce into a saucepan. Mix together to coat vermicelli in sauce. Cook over a low heat until mixture is thoroughly heated through. Serve, garnished with carrot flowers and sesame seeds.

Serves 4.

NOODLES WITH EGGS

375 g (12 oz) buckwheat noodles
2 tablespoons vegetable oil
1 onion, chopped
185 g (6 oz) Chinese leaves, shredded
4 eggs, beaten
3 teaspoons soy sauce
salt and pepper
bay leaf and lemon peel rose, to garnish

In a large saucepan of boiling salted water, cook buckwheat noodles in the same way as spaghetti, until just tender.

Meanwhile, in a heavy saucepan, heat oil. Add onion and cook until soft. Add Chinese leaves and cook until beginning to soften, then stir in beaten eggs. Cook, stirring, for about 1 minute until eggs are beginning to set.

Drain noodles and stir into egg mixture. Add soy sauce and season with salt and pepper. Serve at once, garnished with a bay leaf and lemon peel rose.

Serves 4.

AUBERGINE-FILLED MUSHROOMS

8 mushroom cups, each 5 cm (2 in) across
basil leaves or tomato wedges, to garnish
MARINADE:
3 tomatoes, skinned and seeded
60 ml (2 fl oz/¼ cup) olive oil
¼ teaspoon salt
¼ teaspoon black pepper
1 teaspoon sugar
freshly squeezed juice of 1 orange
4 teaspoons chopped fresh basil
FILLING:
1 aubergine (eggplant)
1 clove garlic, crushed
90 g (3 oz/⅓ cup) cream cheese

Remove stalks from mushrooms. Arrange mushrooms in a dish.

To make marinade, place mushroom stalks in a food processor fitted with a metal blade with tomatoes, oil, salt, pepper, sugar, orange juice and basil and process until smooth.

Spoon marinade into each mushroom cup and pour remainder into dish. Cover with plastic wrap and leave in a cool place for 1 hour.

Meanwhile, preheat oven to 220C (425F/Gas 7). Make the filling, bake aubergine (eggplant) for 15-20 minutes, until skin looks burnt and flesh is tender. Cool, then peel away skin and scrape flesh into food processor.

Add garlic, cream cheese, salt and pepper; process until smooth.

Remove plastic wrap and bake mushrooms for 5 minutes. Spoon aubergine (eggplant) mixture into each cup, then return to the oven for a further 5-8 minutes, until filling has set and the mushrooms are tender.

Serve as a snack or starter, garnished with basil leaves or tomato wedges.

Serves 4.

— CRISPY COATED VEGETABLES —

8 cup mushrooms, halved
2 courgettes (zucchini), cut into 1 cm (½ in) slices
125 g (4 oz) mange tout or dwarf French beans, topped and tailed
1 fennel bulb, broken into bite-size pieces
250 g (8 oz) cauliflower or broccoli, broken into flowerets
vegetable oil for deep frying
lime wedges and fennel sprigs, to garnish
MARINADE:
8 teaspoons chopped fresh basil
2 teaspoons finely grated lime peel
3 teaspoons freshly squeezed lime juice
1 teaspoon finely grated fresh root ginger
1 teaspoon caster sugar
6 teaspoons olive oil
½ teaspoon each salt and black pepper
BATTER:
125 g (4 oz/1 cup) self-raising flour
1 egg, separated

To make marinade, mix basil, lime peel and juice, ginger, sugar, oil, salt and pepper together, stirring well.

Add all vegetables to marinade and turn to coat evenly. Cover with plastic wrap and leave for 1 hour.

To make batter, place flour in a bowl and make a well in centre. Add egg yolk and gradually stir in 155 ml (5 fl oz/⅔) cup water, beating until smooth. Stiffly whisk egg white and fold into batter.

Half-fill a deep-fat frying pan with oil and heat to 180C (350F). Take 1 piece of vegetable at a time and dip into batter to coat evenly, then place in oil. Fry about 12 pieces of vegetable at a time until lightly browned and crisp. Drain well on absorbent kitchen paper. Repeat with rest of vegetables.

Arrange on a serving plate, garnish and serve with a spicy dip or dressing.

Serves 4.

BRIE & FIG TEMPTER

7 g (¼ oz/1½ teaspoons) unsalted butter, softened

1 wholemeal rye crispbread

2-3 small red oakleaf or endive lettuce leaves

3 slices Brie

1 fresh ripe fig, cut into 6 wedges

1 teaspoon fresh lime juice

lime twists and marjoram sprigs, to garnish (optional)

Spread butter over crispbread. Cover with lettuce leaves and press down lightly.

Arrange overlapping slices of Brie, at a slight angle, over crispbread, allowing ends to slightly overlap edges.

Sprinkle fig wedges with lime juice and arrange attractively with cheese. Garnish with twists of lime and sprigs of marjoram, if desired.

Makes 1.

Variations: Light or dark rye bread, sliced diagonally, may be used instead of crispbread, if preferred. Use sliced kiwi fruit, instead of fig, if desired.

ROQUEFORT & GRAPE TREAT

7 g (¼ oz/1½ teaspoons) unsalted butter, softened

1 slice dark rye bread, sliced diagonally

several lamb's lettuce leaves

2-3 slices Roquefort cheese

2-3 neat sprigs of seedless black or green grapes, each containing 2-3 grapes

2 teaspoons thick sour cream

lime twists and chervil sprigs, to garnish

Spread butter over the slice of bread. Cover bread with lamb's lettuce, allowing tips of leaves to overlap edges of bread.

Arrange overlapping slices of Roquefort cheese over lettuce. Add sprigs of grapes to one side and sour cream to other side.

Garnish with lime and chervil.

Makes 1.

Variations: Use any other blue-veined cheese of your choice and arrange over sprigs of watercress instead of lamb's lettuce. Use a spoonful of mayonnaise instead of thick sour cream, if preferred.

GREEK SALAD PITTAS

6 tablespoons olive oil
2 tablespoons lemon juice
1 clove garlic, crushed
¼ teaspoon caster sugar
1 teaspoon chopped fresh oregano
salt and pepper
¼ Cos lettuce, shredded
1 small red onion, sliced and separated into rings
¼ cucumber, sliced
1 beefsteak tomato, quartered and sliced
½ small green pepper (capsicum), seeded and cut into slivers
125 g (4 oz) feta cheese, cut into cubes or fingers
4 large pitta breads
12 black olives, stoned
lemon twists and oregano sprigs, to garnish

In a bowl, whisk together oil, lemon juice, garlic, sugar and oregano. Season with salt and pepper. Add lettuce, onion, cucumber, tomato, green pepper (capsicum) and cheese and toss ingredients lightly together until coated with dressing.

Lightly toast pitta breads. Cut a slice off long edge of each one and carefully open out to form 'pockets'. Generously fill each pitta with salad mixture, allowing mixture to rise above top edge of bread each time.

Add olives to each one and garnish with lemon twists and sprigs of oregano.

Makes 4.

WELSH RAREBITS

30 g (1 oz/6 teaspoons) butter
155 g (5 oz/1¼ cups) Cheddar cheese, grated
1 teaspoon milk
¼ teaspoon dry mustard
few drops Worcestershire sauce
good pinch cayenne pepper
salt
2 crusty slices granary bread
tomato wedges and watercress sprigs, to garnish

Melt 15 g (½ oz/3 teaspoons) butter in a small saucepan. Remove from heat, add cheese, milk, mustard, Worcestershire sauce and cayenne pepper. Season with salt. Heat very gently for a few moments until beginning to melt. Remove from heat.

Toast bread and spread with remaining butter. Spread cheese mixture on top. Cook under a hot grill for 3-4 minutes or until golden and bubbling. Serve hot, garnished with tomato wedges and watercress sprigs.

Makes 2.

FRENCH TOAST FINGERS

1 egg
1 tablespoon milk
2-3 drops Tabasco sauce
2 teaspoons tomato purée (paste)
1 small clove garlic, crushed (optional)
salt and pepper
2 slices mixed grain bread, crusts removed
30 g (1 oz/6 teaspoons) butter
1 slice processed Cheddar cheese
1 small tomato, thinly sliced
1 teaspoon chopped fresh chives
chopped fresh chives, to garnish

In a bowl, beat egg with milk, Tabasco sauce, tomato purée (paste) and garlic, if desired. Season with salt and pepper.

Soak slices of bread in egg mixture. Melt butter in a frying pan. Gently fry soaked bread, turning, until golden and crisp on both sides.

Remove from pan and while still hot cover 1 slice with processed cheese and tomato and sprinkle with chives. Cover with remaining slice of toast and press together lightly.

Cut into 3 fingers and serve hot, garnished along centres with chopped chives.

Makes 3.

Variation: For Sweet French Toast, beat egg with milk, few drops vanilla essence and finely grated rind of 1 small orange. Fry as given above. Sprinkle with a mixture of 1 tablespoon caster or light soft brown sugar and ½ teaspoon ground cinnamon. Cut diagonally into quarters and decorate with orange twists and strawberries.

CREAM CHEESE BITES

4 slices pumpernickel
2 teaspoons thick sour cream or mayonnaise
3 tablespoons very finely chopped fresh parsley
375 g (12 oz) cream cheese
90 g (3 oz/⅓ cup) butter, softened
1 tablespoon tomato purée (paste)
3 pinches cayenne pepper
1-2 teaspoons concentrated curry paste
1 clove garlic, crushed
6 black grapes, halved and seeded
6 green grapes, halved and seeded
small chervil and parsley sprigs, to garnish

Using a 4 cm (1½ in) plain round biscuit cutter, cut out 6 rounds from each slice of pumpernickel. Spread edges of bread rounds lightly with thick sour cream or mayonnaise, then dip into parsley to coat.

In a bowl, mix together cream cheese and butter until soft and well combined. Put half quantity into another bowl. To one bowl, add tomato purée (paste) and cayenne pepper and mix well. To other bowl, add curry paste and garlic and mix.

Put mixtures into 2 piping bags fitted with large star nozzles. Pipe tomato mixture in a swirl over 12 bread rounds and curry mixture onto remaining 12 bread rounds.

Lightly press 6 curry rounds onto 6 tomato rounds, curry sides up, and 6 tomato rounds onto 6 curry rounds, tomato sides up. Place black grapes on tomato toppings and green grapes on curry toppings. Garnish with chervil and parsley.

Makes 12.

Variations: Use white or brown toast rounds instead of pumpernickel and coat buttered edges with poppy seeds. Garnish toppings with walnut or pecan halves, if desired.

PEANUT-BANANA MALTIES

3 thin slices malt bread
2 tablespoons crunchy peanut butter
1 banana
1 tablespoon lemon juice
¼-½ teaspoon ground cinnamon
1 teaspoon light soft brown sugar
60 g (2 oz) full fat soft cheese
2 chunky wedges green or red eating apple, to decorate

Spread 1 slice of malt bread with 1 tablespoon peanut butter. Cut off 2 slices from banana, dip in lemon juice and reserve for decoration. Cut remaining banana in half cross-wise and then into thin lengthwise slices. Dip in lemon juice. Mix together cinnamon and sugar.

Cover peanut butter with half quantity of banana slices and sprinkle with a little cinnamon sugar.

Spread a slice of bread with cheese and place, cheese-side down, over sliced banana. Spread this slice of bread with remaining peanut butter and cover with remaining long slices of banana. Sprinkle with a little cinnamon sugar.

Spread remaining slice of bread with remaining cheese and place over banana.

Press sandwich firmly together and cut diagonally in half. Secure each one with a cocktail stick. Dip wedges of apple into lemon juice. Thread reserved slices of banana and apple wedges onto cocktail sticks. Sprinkle both halves with remaining cinnamon sugar and serve at once.

Makes 2.

TROPICAL TEACAKES

185 g (6 oz) cream cheese
finely grated rind of 1 small lemon
3 tablespoons double (thick) cream
1 teacake
2 kiwi fruit, peeled and thinly sliced
10 blanched almonds, toasted, and 2 maraschino cherries, halved, to decorate

In a bowl, mix cream cheese with lemon rind and cream.

Split and toast teacake halves until lightly golden. Allow to cool, standing upright.

Spread teacake halves with two-thirds of cream cheese mixture. Transfer remaining mixture to a piping bag fitted with a large star nozzle and reserve for decoration.

Arrange overlapping slices of kiwi fruit on top of cheese mixture, reserving 2 slices for decoration. Pipe reserved cream cheese mixture in a rosette in centre of each teacake. Cut reserved slices of kiwi fruit from one side through to centre and arrange in a twist on top of cheese.

Stud cheese with toasted almonds and decorate each side of kiwi fruit twist with maraschino cherry halves.

Makes 2.

EGG & MUSHROOM BENEDICT

2 muffins

125 g (4 oz/½ cup) herb butter (see Note)

4 large flat field mushrooms

4 eggs

6 teaspoons white wine vinegar

1 egg yolk

125 g (4 oz/½ cup) butter, melted

salt and pepper

chervil sprigs, to garnish

Split muffins in half and toast on both sides under a hot grill.

Melt herb butter and generously brush both sides of each mushroom, then place under a hot grill and cook them for 2 minutes on each side.

Bring a large saucepan of water to simmering point and carefully crack the eggs into it. Poach the eggs for 3-4 minutes, then remove them from the pan with a slotted spoon and drain on absorbent kitchen paper while making the sauce.

In a small pan, bring the vinegar and 3 teaspoons water to the boil and reduce by half. Put egg yolk into a blender or food processor and process for 30 seconds, at the same time pouring in the hot vinegar. Then slowly add the melted butter. Season to taste.

Put a mushroom on top of each half muffin, top with an egg and spoon over some of the sauce. Garnish with sprigs of chervil and serve at once.

Serves 4.

Note: Make herb butter by adding 1 tablespoon of finely chopped fresh herbs of your choice to 125 g (4 oz/½ cup) softened butter.

CHEESY DAMPER

375 g (12 oz/3 cups) self-raising flour

1 teaspoon baking powder

¼ teaspoon salt

1 teaspoon sugar

250 ml (8 fl oz/1 cup) milk

2 teaspoons prepared American mustard

60 g (2 oz/½ cup) grated mature Cheddar cheese

185 g (6 oz) double Gloucester cheese with chives

60 g (2 oz/¼ cup) butter

6 teaspoons single (light) cream

2 teaspoons dry sherry

2 teaspoons chopped fresh chives

Preheat the oven to 220C (425F/ Gas 7). Sift flour, baking powder, salt and sugar into a large bowl. Mix together milk and mustard and pour onto the dry ingredients. Mix everything together quickly to form a soft dough.

Put the dough onto a floured baking sheet and press out to make a rough circle about 4 cm (1½ in) thick. Mark into 8 using a sharp knife, sprinkle with Cheddar cheese and bake in the oven for 10 minutes. Lower the oven temperature to 200C (400F/Gas 6) for a further 20 minutes until well risen and golden.

Remove from the oven and allow to cool slightly. Mash together or process in a food processor the double Gloucester cheese, butter, cream, sherry and chives and pile into a pretty dish. Serve the hot damper broken into pieces, with plenty of potted cheese.

Serves 8.

HERB POPOVERS WITH EGG

POPOVERS:

100 g (3½ oz/¾ cup plus 6 teaspoons) plain flour

½ teaspoon celery salt

2 large eggs

250 ml (8 fl oz/1 cup) milk

3 teaspoons butter, melted

2 tablespoons chopped fresh mixed herbs

parsley sprigs, to garnish

FILLING:

60 g (2 oz/¼ cup) butter

6 large eggs, beaten

2 tablespoons chopped fresh mixed herbs

2 tablespoons single (light) cream

salt and pepper

To make the popovers, sift flour and celery salt into a large bowl, add eggs, milk and butter and beat well. Stir in herbs and pour the mixture into 12 well greased deep bun tins.

Place in a cold oven, heat it to 220C (425F/Gas 7) and bake for 30 minutes without opening the oven door during that time.

To make the filling, melt butter in a small saucepan, add the eggs and cook over a low heat, stirring continuously until thickened. Remove from the heat and stir in the herbs, cream and salt and pepper. Serve the popovers with a mound of herby buttered egg. Garnish with sprigs of parsley.

Serves 6.

AVOCADO & CHEESE OMELETTE

4 large eggs

15 g (½ oz/6 teaspoons) grated Parmesan cheese

30 g (1 oz/6 teaspoons) butter

1 small avocado pear

3 teaspoons thick sour cream

salt and pepper

pinch freshly grated nutmeg

60 g (2 oz) camembert cheese, diced

parsley sprigs and grated Parmesan cheese, to garnish

Beat eggs and Parmesan cheese together in a large bowl. Melt half the butter in a 17.5 cm (7 in) omelette pan and pour in half the egg mixture.

Cut the avocado in half. Slice one half thinly into long fingers. Mash the other half with the sour cream and salt and pepper and nutmeg; stir in the camembert.

Arrange half the avocado fingers in a fan shape on top of the omelette and top with half the camembert mixture. Put under a hot grill for 1 minute until the cheese melts, then fold the omelette in half and tip onto a warmed plate.

Garnish with sprigs of parsley and Parmesan cheese and serve at once. Make the remaining omelette in the same way.

Serves 2.

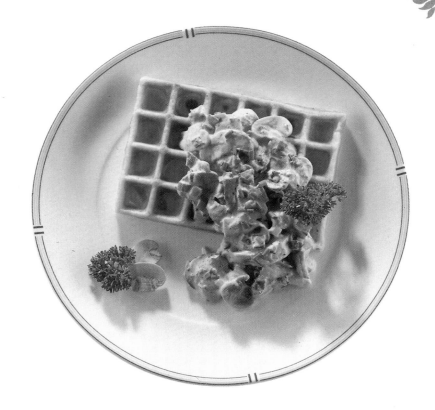

BUCK RAREBIT

125 g (4 oz/1 cup) grated Cheddar cheese
15 g (½ oz/3 teaspoons) butter
½ teaspoon dry mustard
6 teaspoons beer
salt and pepper
3 wholemeal muffins, split and toasted
6 eggs
3 tablespoons mayonnaise
3 tablespoons chopped watercress
watercress sprigs and lemon slices, to garnish

Put cheese, butter, mustard, beer and salt and pepper to taste into a saucepan and heat until the mixture combines into a sauce.

Allow to cool slightly, then pour onto the toasted muffins and cook under a hot grill until golden and bubbly. Poach the eggs in plenty of water, then remove with a slotted spoon and place on top of each muffin half.

Put mayonnaise and watercress into a blender or food processor and blend until smooth. Top each egg with a spoonful of mayonnaise. Garnish with sprigs of watercress and slices of lemon and serve the muffins at once.

Serves 6.

POTATO WAFFLES

185 g (6 oz) mashed potato
60 ml (2 fl oz/¼ cup) hot milk
6 teaspoons plain flour
30 g (1 oz/6 teaspoons) butter, melted
celery salt and pepper
2 eggs, beaten
45 g (1½ oz/9 teaspoons) butter
6 spring onions, chopped
375 g (12 oz) mixed mushrooms
315 ml (10 fl oz/1¼ cups) thick sour cream
1 tablespoon chopped fresh parsley
chopped chives and parsley sprigs, to garnish

In a bowl, beat potato, milk, flour and melted butter together until smooth, then season with celery salt and pepper. Add the eggs and mix well together.

Heat an electric waffle iron and brush with oil. Fill one half with potato batter, clamp down the lid and cook for 2-3 minutes until the steam ceases to escape and the waffles are golden and crisp. Remove from the iron and keep warm. Repeat until all the batter is used up.

Melt butter in a saucepan and fry spring onions and mushrooms until slightly softened, add cream and bring to the boil stirring continuously until thick. Stir in the parsley.

Serve the waffles topped with creamed mushrooms and garnished with chopped chives and sprigs of parsley.

Serves 4.

MUSHROOM KNAPSACKS

4 sheets filo pastry
45 g (1½ oz/9 teaspoons) butter, melted
250 g (8 oz) button mushrooms
82 g (2¾ oz) Boursin cheese
chives, to garnish

Preheat the oven to 220C (425F/ Gas 7). Brush 2 sheets of filo pastry with butter and lay the other 2 sheets of pastry on top of them. Cut each double sheet into about twelve 7.5 cm (3 in) squares.

Remove stalks from mushrooms and fill cavities with ¼ teaspoon-fuls of Boursin cheese. Put each mushroom, cheese side up, into the centre of a square of pastry and bring up the edges to enclose the mushroom completely, leaving the pastry edges pointing upwards.

Brush tops of pastry with butter and bake in the oven for 5 minutes until crisp and golden. Remove them from the oven and allow to cool slightly.

Tie a single chive around the top of each bundle and serve them while still warm.

Makes about 24.

MUSHROOM ROULADE

60 g (2 oz / ¼ cup) herb butter (see page 80)
375 g (12 oz) mixed mushrooms, finely chopped
4 teaspoons plain flour
4 large eggs, separated
3 tablespoons chopped fresh parsley
155 g (5 oz) Boursin cheese
185 g (6 oz) cottage cheese
2 teaspoons chopped fresh chives
4 teaspoons finely grated Parmesan cheese
parsley sprigs, to garnish

Preheat the oven to 200C (400F/ Gas 6). Melt butter in a large frying pan and gently cook mush-rooms for 5-7 minutes until softened. Add flour and bring to the boil, stirring continuously until thick. Remove from the heat and leave to cool slightly.

Whisk egg whites until stiff. Beat egg yolks into mushroom mixture and fold in egg whites and 2 tablespoons of the chopped parsley. Pour into a greased, lined 30 x 22.5 cm (12 x 9 in) swiss roll tin and bake in the oven for 12-15 minutes. Remove from the oven and leave to cool. Meanwhile, prepare the filling.

Beat together Boursin, cottage cheese and chives. Sprinkle a sheet of non-stick baking paper with Parmesan cheese and remaining chopped parsley. Turn roulade out onto the paper and spread with the cheese mixture. Roll up like a swiss roll and transfer to a long serving dish. Serve thick slices garnished with sprigs of parsley.

Serves 4-6.

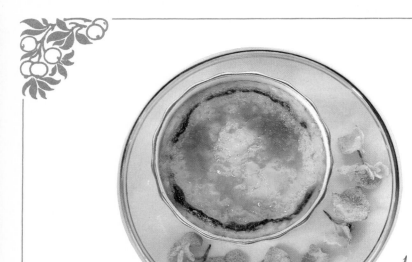

CRÈME BRÛLÉE

CITRUS FLUMMERY

4 egg yolks
2½ teaspoons caster sugar
pinch of cornflour
625 ml (20 fl oz/2½ cups) whipping cream
2 vanilla pods
frosted flowers, to decorate, if desired

CARAMEL TOPPING: caster sugar

In a large bowl, beat egg yolks lightly with sugar and cornflour.

75 ml (2½ fl oz/⅓ cup) frozen concentrated orange and passion fruit juice
315 ml (10 fl oz/1¼ cups) double (thick) cream
1 egg white
30 g (1 oz/5 teaspoons) caster sugar (see Note)
orange wedges and passion fruit, to decorate
langues de chat biscuits, to serve

Thaw concentrated fruit juice and measure out required quantity. (Use remainder as a drink, making up with water.) In a bowl, whip cream to soft peaks.

Put cream into a saucepan. With a sharp knife, split open vanilla pods and scrape seeds into cream. Bring almost to boiling point, then pour onto yolks, beating all the time. Pour into top of a double boiler, or a bowl set over a pan of simmering water, and cook over medium heat until mixture thickens sufficiently to coat the back of spoon. Pour into shallow gratin dish. Leave to cool, then chill in the refrigerator overnight.

Add juice gradually, continuing to whip cream, until fairly thick.

Two hours before serving, heat grill to very high. Cover surface of pudding thickly and evenly with sugar and place under grill until the sugar has caramellized. Chill for 2 hours. Decorate with frosted flowers, if desired.

Serves 4-6.

Note: The best vanilla pods are coated in white crystals and are very expensive. All vanilla pods can be washed after use and used again. Store them in a dry place.

In a separate bowl, whisk egg white until stiff. Whisk in sugar, then fold into creamy mixture. Spoon into individual glasses and chill for 1 hour. Decorate with orange wedges and passion fruit. Serve with the biscuits.

Serves 4-6.

Note: Flavour the sugar for this and other desserts and cakes by keeping it in a jar with a vanilla pod. This will give the sugar a strong vanilla flavour.

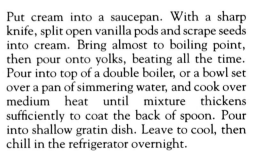

GOOSEBERRY ICE CREAM

750 g (1½ lb) gooseberries, thawed if frozen
125 g (4 oz/½ cup) caster sugar
3 egg yolks
1 small avocado
315 ml (10 fl oz/1¼ cups) whipping cream
gooseberries, leaves or borage flowers, to decorate, if desired

Put gooseberries into a saucepan with 2 tablespoons water and cook over a low heat until soft. Purée in a blender or food processor, then sieve to remove pips. Set aside to cool.

Put sugar into a saucepan with 2 tablespoons water, dissolve over medium heat, then boil syrup to thread stage, 110C (225F) on a sugar thermometer. In a bowl, beat egg yolks lightly, then pour syrup onto them and whisk until mixture is thick and mousse-like. Peel avocado, discard stone and mash flesh. Mix into gooseberry purée. Whip cream and fold into egg mixture with purée. Turn into rigid plastic container and freeze for 1-2 hours until beginning to be firm.

Remove from freezer and beat well. Freeze until firm. Transfer to refrigerator to soften for 30 minutes before serving. Serve in scoops in chilled glasses. Decorate each one with gooseberries, leaves or borage flowers.

Serves 4-6.

Note: Avocado gives this ice-cream a lovely texture. Its taste is not discernible.
    When cooking acidic fruits, such as gooseberries, do not use an aluminium pan. The fruit will taste metallic.

NUTTY BROWN BREAD CREAM

60 g (2 oz/½ cup) hazelnuts
75 g (2½ oz/1¼ cups) fresh brown breadcrumbs
30 g (1 oz/2 tablespoons) demerara sugar
2 egg whites
90 g (3 oz/⅓ cup) caster sugar
315 ml (10 fl oz/1¼ cups) whipping cream
1-2 drops vanilla essence

Toast hazelnuts evenly, cool, then grind coarsely in a coffee grinder. Mix with breadcrumbs and demerara sugar in a bowl.

Tip crumb mixture onto a baking sheet and spread out evenly. Grill under medium-hot grill, turning and shaking, until brown. Leave to cool. Whisk egg whites in a large bowl, until stiff. Sprinkle in sugar and whisk for a further 2 minutes. In a separate bowl, whip cream with vanilla essence to soft peaks, then fold into egg whites with all but 1 tablespoon of breadcrumb mixture.

Spoon mixture into 6 glasses and chill until ready to serve. Sprinkle with reserved crumb mixture just before serving.

Serves 6.

Note: This mixture makes a delicious ice cream; simply turn the finished cream into a plastic container and freeze.

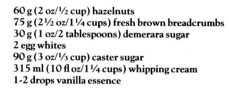

OEUFS À LA NEIGE

4 eggs, separated
scant ½ teaspoon cornflour
90 g (3 oz/⅓ cup) caster sugar
125 ml (4 fl oz/½ cup) milk
315 ml (10 fl oz/1¼ cups) single (light) cream
1 vanilla pod
1 tablespoon orange flower water
1 tablespoon toasted, flaked almonds
orange peel strips, to decorate

In a bowl, cream egg yolks with cornflour and one-third of the caster sugar. Place milk, cream and vanilla pod in a saucepan and scald (bring to near boiling point).

Pour the hot milk over the egg yolks, whisking all the time. Place bowl over a saucepan of simmering water and cook gently, stirring, until it is the consistency of double cream. Cool, remove vanilla pod and stir in orange flower water. In a large bowl, whisk egg whites until stiff, add remaining sugar and whisk again.

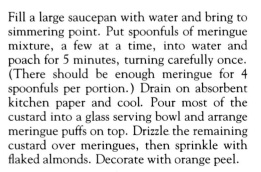

Fill a large saucepan with water and bring to simmering point. Put spoonfuls of meringue mixture, a few at a time, into water and poach for 5 minutes, turning carefully once. (There should be enough meringue for 4 spoonfuls per portion.) Drain on absorbent kitchen paper and cool. Pour most of the custard into a glass serving bowl and arrange meringue puffs on top. Drizzle the remaining custard over meringues, then sprinkle with flaked almonds. Decorate with orange peel.

Serves 4.

CREAMY CRANBERRY FOOL

185 g (6 oz) cranberries, fresh or frozen, thawed if frozen
90 ml (3 fl oz/⅓ cup) orange juice
185 g (6 oz/¾ cup) caster sugar
315 ml (10 fl oz/1¼ cups) whipping cream
grated orange peel, to decorate

Put cranberries into a saucepan with orange juice and sugar and simmer for about 10 minutes, until berries pop. Set aside to cool.

When cranberries are cold, rub through a fine metal sieve, using a wooden spoon. In a large bowl, whip cream until stiff and fold in purée. Chill until ready to serve.

Serve fool in individual glasses topped with a little grated orange peel.

Serves 4.

Note: Substitute 250 g (8 oz) damson for the cranberries. Cook them with 3 tablespoons water and omit orange juice.

CARAMEL RICE

QUEEN OF PUDDINGS

75 g (2½ oz/⅓ cup) pudding rice, washed and drained
625 ml (20 fl oz/2½ cups) milk
1 vanilla pod
125 ml (4 fl oz/½ cup) single (light) cream
juice of 1 orange
caster sugar
orange peel strips, to decorate

Put rice, milk and vanilla pod into a saucepan and simmer on a very low heat for 45-60 minutes, until rice is soft and creamy.

500 ml (16 fl oz/2 cups) milk
155 ml (5 fl oz/⅔ cup) single cream
grated peel of 1 small lemon
90 g (3 oz/1½ cups) fresh white breadcrumbs
45 g (1½ oz/9 teaspoons) butter
250 g (8 oz/1¼ cups) caster sugar
3 small eggs, separated
3 tablespoons raspberry jam

Preheat oven to 180C (350F/Gas 4). Butter a 1.25 litre (40 fl oz/5 cup) pie dish. Put milk, cream and lemon peel in a saucepan.

Remove vanilla pod from mixture and stir in cream and orange juice. Spoon into an ovenproof gratin or soufflé dish. Leave to go cold, then refrigerate until ready to serve.

Heat milk mixture gently for 5 minutes, then remove from heat and leave to infuse for 5 minutes. Put breadcrumbs, butter and one-quarter of the sugar into a bowl and pour the warm milk on top. Stir until butter and sugar have dissolved. In a small bowl, beat egg yolks, then stir them into breadcrumb mixture. Turn into prepared pie dish and bake for 45-50 minutes, until set. Remove from oven and cool slightly. Warm raspberry jam in a pan and spread over pudding.

Cover top of pudding thickly and evenly with caster sugar. Place under a very hot grill until sugar topping has caramellized. Serve at once, decorated with orange peel.

Serves 4.

Note: Chill the pudding again before serving, if preferred, but serve within 2 hours.

Lower oven temperature to 160C (325F/Gas 3). In a large bowl, whisk egg whites until stiff, then fold in remaining sugar. Pile this meringue mixture onto pudding and return to oven for about 20 minutes, until meringue is crisp and golden. Serve warm or cold.

Serves 4.

Note: Sieve the warmed raspberry jam to remove pips, if desired.

— BREAD & BUTTER PUDDING —

125 g (4 oz/³⁄₄ cup) sultanas and currants, mixed
8 slices thin white bread, buttered
30 g (1 oz/2 tablespoons) candied fruit, chopped
caster sugar for sprinkling

CUSTARD: 1 egg yolk
315 ml (10 fl oz/1¼ cups) milk
155 ml (5 fl oz/²⁄₃ cup) single (light) cream
1 vanilla pod
1 teaspoon caster sugar

Put sultanas and currants into a bowl and cover with water. Leave to swell. Preheat oven to 180C (350F/Gas 4). Grease a 1 litre (32 fl oz/4 cup) pie dish.

Cut crusts from bread and sandwich 4 slices together. Cut into 6 pieces and place in prepared pie dish. Drain fruit and scatter over bread with chopped candied fruit. Top with remaining bread, butter side up.

Put egg yolk in a medium bowl. Put milk, cream, vanilla pod and sugar into a saucepan and bring almost to boiling point. Pour over egg, stir, then strain into pie dish, pouring down sides so top slices of bread are not soaked. Stand for 30 minutes, then sprinkle with caster sugar and place in a roasting tin. Pour in boiling water to come halfway up sides of dish and bake in the oven for 45-50 minutes, until top is golden brown.

Serves 4.

— STRAWBERRY SHORTCAKE —

125 g (4 oz/½ cup) butter, softened
60 g (2 oz/¼ cup) caster sugar
155 g (5 oz/1¼ cups) plain flour
30 g (1 oz/3 tablespoons) cornflour
375 g (12 oz) strawberries, hulled, and halved if large
3 tablespoons redcurrant jelly
315 ml (10 fl oz/1¼ cups) whipping cream

Preheat oven to 180C (350F/Gas 4). In a bowl, cream butter and sugar together until light and fluffy. Sift flour and cornflour together into creamy mixture and stir to make a firm dough.

Wrap in foil and chill for 30 minutes. Put dough onto a baking sheet and pat or roll it to a circle, about 1 cm (½ in) thick. Prick all over with a fork and bake in the oven for about 20 minutes, until lightly golden. Leave on baking sheet to cool.

Carefully transfer the shortcake to a serving plate and cover with the strawberries. Melt redcurrant jelly in a small saucepan and brush it over the strawberries. Whip cream stiffly in a bowl and use to pipe a border round edge of shortcake. Serve within 1 hour.

Serves 6-8.

ATHOLL BROSE

45 g (1½ oz/3 tablespoons) medium oatmeal
60 g (2 oz/⅓ cup) whole blanched almonds
315 ml (10 fl oz/1¼ cups) double (thick) cream
60 ml (2 fl oz/¼ cup) whisky
90 g (3 oz/¼ cup) orange flower honey
1 tablespoon lemon juice

Toast oatmeal under a medium-hot grill until evenly browned. Toast the almonds in the same way, then chop them finely.

In a large bowl, whip cream to soft peaks, then gradually whisk in whisky, honey and lemon juice.

Fold oatmeal and half the chopped almonds into creamy mixture and spoon into 4 glasses. Chill in the refrigerator. When ready to serve, sprinkle remaining almonds on top of each pudding.

Serves 4.

Note: This traditional Scottish dessert is very rich and is perfect for a dinner party.

YOGURT FUDGE CREAM

315 ml (10 fl oz/1¼ cups) whipping cream
250 g (8 oz/1 cup) natural yogurt
250 g (8 oz/1½ cups) brown sugar
fresh strawberries or raspberries, to serve, if desired

In a large bowl, whip cream to stiff peaks. Fold in the yogurt.

Half fill 4 glasses with the creamy mixture. Sprinkle with about one-third of the sugar. Spoon remaining creamy mixture on top of the sugar, then pile on remaining sugar.

Chill in the refrigerator overnight. Serve puddings on their own, or with fresh strawberries or raspberries, if desired.

Serves 4.

Note: The brown sugar dissolves and forms a fudgy layer in these puddings. They must be prepared a day in advance to allow for this.

DACQUOISE

CHERRY CLAFOUTI

155 g (5 oz/1 cup) whole blanched almonds
5 egg whites
315 g (10 oz/1½ cups) caster sugar
185 g (6 oz/2¾ cups) dried apricots
juice of 1 lemon
375 ml (12 fl oz/1½ cups) whipping cream
toasted flaked almonds, to decorate

Preheat oven to 150C (300F/Gas 2). Line a baking sheet with silicone paper. Toast almonds under a medium grill to brown evenly. Cool, then grind finely in a coffee grinder or food processor. Set aside.

In a large bowl, whisk egg whites until stiff, but not dry. Sprinkle over 2 tablespoons of the caster sugar and whisk for a further 1 minute. Fold in remaining sugar with ground almonds, using a metal spoon. Spoon meringue onto lined baking sheet and spread evenly to a 25 cm (10 in) circle. Bake in the oven for 1½-2 hours, until dry and biscuit coloured. Peel off paper and cool meringue on a wire rack.

Put apricots and lemon juice into a saucepan, cover with water and simmer over medium heat for about 30 minutes, until tender. Cool, then purée apricots with a little cooking liquid in a blender or food processor to make a thick purée. Whip cream stiffly and fold half the purée into it. Pile onto meringue and dribble remaining purée, thinned with a little more cooking liquid, over top. Sprinkle with flaked almonds to decorate.

Serves 6-8.

750 g (1½ lb) stoned black cherries, fresh or frozen,
thawed if frozen
90 g (3 oz/¾ cup) plain flour
pinch of salt
3 eggs
90 g (3 oz/⅓ cup) caster sugar
500 ml (16 fl oz/2 cups) milk
1 tablespoon cherry brandy or kirsch
icing sugar, to serve

Preheat oven to 200C (400F/Gas 6). Drain the cherries, if thawed. Butter a 1.25 litre (40 fl oz/5 cup) pie dish and put cherries in it.

Sift flour and salt together onto a plate. In a large bowl, beat eggs with sugar until creamy, then fold in flour. Warm milk slightly in a saucepan over a low heat and stir into egg mixture with cherry brandy or kirsch. Beat well to make batter smooth, then pour the batter over the cherries.

Bake in the oven for 30 minutes, until batter is set and golden. Serve warm, dusted with icing sugar.

Serves 6.

Note: Fresh cherries can taste a little bland when cooked. Add 1-2 drops almond essence to improve the flavour, if desired.

CHOCOLATE PEARS

60 g (2 oz) amaretti biscuits
3-4 tablespoons Cointreau
125 g (4 oz) plain (dark) chocolate
3 tablespoons strong black coffee
1 tablespoon orange juice
30 g (1 oz/6 teaspoons) butter
2 eggs, separated
4 ripe pears

Put amaretti biscuits into a bowl, pour over liqueur, then crush biscuits to rough crumbs using end of a rolling pin.

Melt chocolate with coffee and orange juice in the top of a double boiler or a bowl set over a saucepan of simmering water. When smooth, remove from heat and beat in butter and egg yolks. In a separate bowl, whisk egg whites until stiff and fold chocolate mixture into them. Set aside. Peel pears, leaving them whole with stalks intact. Hollow out as much core as possible from the base and fill cavity with crumb mixture.

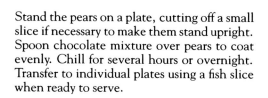

Stand the pears on a plate, cutting off a small slice if necessary to make them stand upright. Spoon chocolate mixture over pears to coat evenly. Chill for several hours or overnight. Transfer to individual plates using a fish slice when ready to serve.

Serves 4.

MINTY CHOCOLATE MOUSSE

185 g (6 oz) plain (dark) chocolate
315 ml (10 fl oz/1¼ cups) double (thick) cream
1 egg
pinch of salt
few drops peppermint essence

TO DECORATE: mint leaves
1 small egg white
caster sugar
grated chocolate

Break chocolate into small pieces and put into a blender or food processor fitted with a metal blade.

Heat cream in a small saucepan until almost boiling. Pour over chocolate and blend for 1 minute. Add egg, salt and peppermint essence and blend for 1 minute more. Pour into individual ramekin dishes or chocolate cups and refrigerate overnight.

To make the decoration, wash and dry mint leaves. Lightly whisk egg white in a shallow bowl and dip in mint leaves to cover. Dip them into caster sugar, shake off any excess and leave to harden on greaseproof paper. Place on each mousse just before serving and sprinkle with grated chocolate.

Serves 4-6.

Note: Peppermint essence has a very strong flavour; use it sparingly.

APPLE CHARLOTTE

750 g (1½ lb) eating apples
grated peel of 1 lemon
90 g (3 oz/½ cup) brown sugar
125 g (4 oz/½ cup) butter
155 g (5 oz/2½ cups) coarse fresh breadcrumbs
apple slices and mint sprigs, to decorate

Peel, core and slice apples. Put into a saucepan with grated lemon peel, 60 g (2 oz/⅓ cup) of the sugar and 30 g (1 oz/6 teaspoons) of the butter. Simmer, covered, over a low heat until soft. Beat until pulpy.

Melt remaining butter in a frying pan and fry breadcrumbs until golden brown, stirring constantly to prevent burning. Stir in remaining sugar and leave to cool.

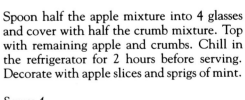

Spoon half the apple mixture into 4 glasses and cover with half the crumb mixture. Top with remaining apple and crumbs. Chill in the refrigerator for 2 hours before serving. Decorate with apple slices and sprigs of mint.

Serves 4.

SUMMER PUDDING

500 g (1 lb) redcurrants and blackcurrants, mixed
juice of ½ orange
125 g (4 oz/½ cup) caster sugar
250 g (8 oz) raspberries
12-16 slices thin white bread
extra raspberries, if desired, and whipping cream, to
  serve

Put currants into a saucepan with orange juice and sugar and cook over a low heat, stirring occasionally, until juicy and just tender. Gently stir in raspberries, then set aside to cool.

Cut crusts from bread. From 6 slices, cut circles the same size as the top of small ramekin dishes or dariole moulds. Use remaining bread to line 6 ramekin dishes or dariole moulds, overlapping bread to line dishes completely. Strain fruit, reserving juices, and spoon fruit into bread-lined dishes, pressing down quite firmly. Cover with bread circles. Pour some of the reserved juice into dishes to soak bread. Put a small weight on top of each pudding.

Chill puddings and remaining juice, for several hours or overnight. When ready to serve, turn puddings out onto individual plates and spoon a little of the reserved juices around them. Top with the extra raspberries, if desired. Whip cream lightly and dot a small amount in the juice and serve the remaining cream separately.

Serves 6.

FLAMING FRUIT SALAD

BAKED DEMELZA APPLES

500 g (1 lb/7½ cups) mixed dried fruit, such as prunes,
  apricots, figs, apples, pears and peaches
2 tablespoons sherry
juice of ½ lemon
2 tablespoons clear honey
½ cinnamon stick
4 tablespoons brandy
90 g (3 oz/¾ cup) toasted almond flakes
60 g (2 oz/½ cup) walnuts, coarsely chopped
chilled single (light) cream or ice cream, to serve

Soak fruit overnight in 625 ml (20 fl oz/2½
cups) water and the sherry.

60 g (2 oz/⅓ cup) mixed raisins and sultanas
5 tablespoons ginger wine, Madeira or sweet sherry
4 large cooking apples
90 g (3 oz/¾ cup) toasted, flaked almonds
1-2 tablespoons marmalade
chilled whipped cream, to serve

Preheat oven to 180C (350F/Gas 4). Put
raisins and sultanas into a small bowl and add
ginger wine, Madeira or sherry. Leave to soak
for several hours.

Put fruit and soaking liquid into a saucepan
with lemon juice, honey and cinnamon stick.
Cover and simmer on a low heat until fruit is
just tender. Discard cinnamon stick, transfer
fruit to serving dish and keep warm.

Wash and dry apples, but do not peel.
Remove core using an apple corer and score a
line around each apple. Stand the apples in
an ovenproof dish. Drain dried fruit,
reserving liquid. Mix fruit with almonds and
marmalade in a bowl, then fill the apple
cavities with this mixture, pushing it down
firmly. Pour strained liquid over apples.

In a small pan, heat brandy and set alight.
While still flaming, pour it over the fruit.
Scatter with almonds and walnuts and serve
immediately, with cream or ice cream.

Serves 5-6.

Note: The effect of flaming brandy is to burn
off the alcohol and so concentrate the
flavour. It is important to warm brandy first or
it will not set alight.

Bake the apples in the oven for 45-60
minutes, until soft. Pile a spoonful of
whipped cream on top of each apple and
serve immediately.

Serves 4.

CREAM CHEESE STRUDEL

NECTARINE BAKLAVA

75 g (2½ oz / ¾ cup) hazelnuts
250 g (8 oz) cream or curd cheese
2 tablespoons caster sugar
1 egg
grated peel of 1 lemon
5 sheets filo pastry, thawed if frozen
60 g (2 oz / ¼ cup) butter, melted
icing sugar for dusting

10 sheets filo pastry, thawed if frozen
155 g (5 oz/⅔ cup) butter, melted
220 g (7 oz/1¾ cups) chopped mixed nuts
1½ teaspoons ground cinnamon
8 tablespoons caster sugar
juice and grated peel of 2 lemons
1 tablespoon orange flower water
4 nectarines
icing sugar, to decorate

Preheat oven to 200C (400F/Gas 6). Grease a baking sheet. Toast hazelnuts under medium grill to brown evenly. Set aside to cool, then chop.

Preheat oven to 180C (350F/Gas 4). Cut pastry sheets in half, and each half into 4.

In a bowl, beat cheese with sugar, egg and lemon peel until smooth. Beat in hazelnuts. Place a sheet of pastry on greased baking sheet, keeping remainder covered with a damp tea towel. Brush with melted butter and place another sheet on top. Layer all 5 sheets of pastry on top of one another, brushing each one with melted butter.

Working quickly, brush one cut sheet of pastry with melted butter. Line 8 individual 10 cm (4 in) Yorkshire pudding tins with one piece of pastry each. Brush 3 more cut sheets with butter and lay the pieces in the tins, so each tin has 4 pieces overlapping each other at different angles. Mix nuts, cinnamon and half the sugar, and spread half this mixture over pastry. Cover with 2 more layers of pastry, brushed with butter, then top with remaining nut mixture. Cover with rest of pastry, brushed with butter.

Spoon cheese mixture in a line down centre of pastry and fold either short end over the filling. Roll up pastry, round filling, and turn it on baking sheet, so join is underneath. Brush top of strudel with remaining butter and bake in the oven for 25-30 minutes, until golden brown and flaky. Dust with icing sugar and serve warm, cut in diagonal slices.

Serves 4-6.

Press down pastry in tins and bake in the oven for 20-25 minutes, until golden brown. Meanwhile, dissolve remaining sugar in lemon juice over low heat. Stir in lemon peel and orange flower water. Bring to boil and simmer for 3 minutes. Cool slightly. Slice nectarines into syrup, turning them carefully to coat. Spoon into centre of pastries and dust edges with icing sugar. Serve lukewarm or cold, when pastries have absorbed some of the syrup.

Serves 8.

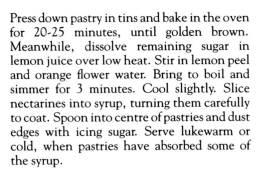

TARTE FRANÇAISE

AUSTRIAN CURD CHEESECAKE

410 g (13 oz) puff pastry, thawed if frozen
1 egg yolk, beaten
6 tablespoons apricot jam, sieved
2 tablespoons lemon juice
about 750 g (1½ lb) mixed fresh fruit, such as grapes,
   strawberries and/or raspberries and bananas

Preheat oven to 220C (425F/Gas 7). Roll out pastry to a 30 x 20 cm (12 x 8 in) rectangle. Fold pastry in half, to a 15 x 20 cm (6 x 8 in) rectangle. Cut a rectangle from folded edge, 4 cm (1½ in) in from outside edges.

60 g (2 oz / ¼ cup) butter, softened
140 g (4½ oz / ⅔ cup) caster sugar
280 g (9 oz) curd cheese, sieved
2 eggs, separated
60 g (2 oz / ½ cup) ground almonds
60 g (2 oz / ⅓ cup) fine semolina
juice and grated peel of 1 small lemon
icing sugar

Preheat oven to 190C (375F/Gas 5). Butter a 20 cm (8 in) cake tin and dust out with flour. In a large bowl, cream butter, sugar and cheese until soft and fluffy.

Unfold middle section and roll out to same size as 'frame' – 30 x 20 cm (12 x 8 in). Place on a baking sheet, dampen edges with water, then unfold 'frame' and place carefully on top of pastry rectangle. Press edges of pastry together, then 'knock up' using a blunt knife. Mark a pattern on frame and brush with beaten egg yolk. Prick centre of case all over.

Beat egg yolks into mixture, then fold in almonds, semolina and lemon juice and peel. In a separate bowl, whisk egg whites stiffly and carefully fold into the cheese mixture.

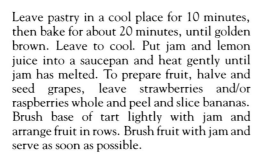

Leave pastry in a cool place for 10 minutes, then bake for about 20 minutes, until golden brown. Leave to cool. Put jam and lemon juice into a saucepan and heat gently until jam has melted. To prepare fruit, halve and seed grapes, leave strawberries and/or raspberries whole and peel and slice bananas. Brush base of tart lightly with jam and arrange fruit in rows. Brush fruit with jam and serve as soon as possible.

Serves 6.

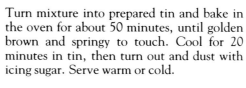

Turn mixture into prepared tin and bake in the oven for about 50 minutes, until golden brown and springy to touch. Cool for 20 minutes in tin, then turn out and dust with icing sugar. Serve warm or cold.

Serves 6.

Note: For a pretty pattern, place a doily on the cake, then dust with icing sugar. Remove doily and serve.